AVOID EXCEL HORROR STORIES

How to excel at creating reliable, user-friendly spreadsheets

Gary Knott

Avoid Excel Horror Stories

How to excel at creating reliable, user-friendly spreadsheets

© 2021, Gary Knott

Credit for the author photo: Yvonne Ploenes

ISBN (e-book): 9 783982 322704
ISBN (print): 9 783982 322711

Table of Contents

Preface

Anyone who knows me knows: I love using spreadsheets. I first encountered them around 1991 when working at Deloitte in England (it was called Touche Ross back then) as an auditor and studying for my Chartered Accountant exams. I remember it well even now... a small screen with green text on a black background running Lotus 1-2-3 for MS-DOS. We later moved on to portable machines with orange-on-black screens and we even got a mouse thrown in. The old screens were terrible, and the mouse pointer often disappeared due to early screen technology. These were portable computers, but large, clunky and relatively heavy – I called them sewing machines. But still, they had Lotus 1-2-3. It only had one sheet (multiple sheets came many years later), but I could use it for all kinds of analysis in my work and could even produce graphs automatically... wow! No more pencil and paper.

I was an enthusiastic user and got stuck into learning how to use it well. Soon colleagues started asking me for help. Over the coming years, I continued to use spreadsheets in my work and later migrated to Excel. I also learnt more about good and bad ways of doing things in spreadsheets. Some of these appeared obvious to me – have a clear layout for example – while others – like master checks – I had to learn and then integrate into my daily way of working.

Sometimes I saw how others were working in Excel and it was often a shock. Messy, unclear sheets, some of them as brightly coloured as a Christmas tree, as if the aim were to divert attention from the content, which was often terrible. Not only were such spreadsheets hard to understand and use but it was also little surprise to discover that they often contained errors. This discovery was further substantiated when I started performing model reviews of client spreadsheets. In large companies, the spreadsheets were often above-average in quality, but the average is sadly not a good standard. So, when I started informally helping and later formally teaching others on developing and using spreadsheets, it became my passion to teach them about golden rules and best practice. In fact, Gary's Golden Ground Rules became a little bit famous at Deloitte and upon leaving the company in 2015, to set up on my own, I received as a parting gift a glass plaque with my (at that time three) Golden Ground Rules engraved upon it. It still proudly stands in my office.

Years later, the passion still burns. It is further enflamed whenever I read of yet another spreadsheet error which has caused a loss of money, time, reputation or all three. And so, I decided to write this book to help spreadsheet developers and users do things better.

Introduction

'Tis impossible to be sure of anything but death
and taxes and spreadsheet errors.'
With apologies to Christopher Bullock, author (1716)

EXCEL IS A FANTASTIC TOOL

I love using Excel – it is very flexible and allows you to report and analyse all kinds of data and plan almost anything with numbers from simple budgets for the home up to complex planning models for international corporations. But its very strength is also its Achilles heel: you can do what you want and that includes creating messy spreadsheets that are hard to understand, hard to use and full of errors. I know this because I have used and reviewed hundreds of Excel files over the years and I have seen the horrible truth. But it doesn't have to be like that.

I am an ardent developer, user and advocate of best practice in Excel. I am convinced, that if you follow the best practice guidelines explained in this book, you too can learn 'how to excel' and will be able to **create spreadsheets which are easier to use, flexible and, above all, reliable.**

But before we dive into the detail, let's take a quick look at the background to see why we cannot just leave developers and users of spreadsheets to their own devices, fully untrained.

Note: In this book I use the terms 'spreadsheet', 'workbook', and 'model' to cover all types of usage. I focus on Microsoft Excel, which is the most commonly used software, but the principles can be applied to other spreadsheet packages as well.

EXCEL IS EVERYWHERE

Well, practically everywhere.

Wherever data is being analysed and reported, projects or entire businesses are being planned, strategic options are being assessed or companies are being valued, you are highly likely to find Excel being used. In fact, I bet you won't find a single accounting, controlling, management reporting, finance or M&A department in a company of any size where Excel is not the tool of choice for these tasks, or at least in common use. Even in other departments such as sales and marketing, purchasing, logistics or human resources, Excel is also a commonly used tool.

A report into spreadsheet use in the UK **(F1F9 CDS)** found that in 78% of British businesses, key financial decisions are supported by spreadsheets. Why is that and just what are they used for? I am glad you asked...

WHY ARE SPREADSHEETS USED SO MUCH?

Availability – 'everyone' has Excel: most company employees and many private users already have it installed as part of Microsoft Office on their computer.

Ease of use & flexibility – it is relatively easy to use for many simple tasks and, in contrast to other software packages (e.g., for planning), you are not restricted to what the standard software enables and allows.

Data – actual data can be exported from many systems in Excel-format to analyse or use as a basis for planning.

These advantages are incredible and lead to spreadsheets being used for all sorts of tasks.

WHAT EXACTLY ARE SPREADSHEETS USED FOR?

Spreadsheet usage is wide and varied, but the main uses can be split into the following categories.

Simple lists

This could be a list of attendees at a conference or training session, or a list of company approved hotels. Excel is simple to use, and the columns facilitate the recording of relevant details for each entry. This kind of use seems to be surprisingly commonplace. After the Enron scandal, an analysis of nearly 16,000 spreadsheets in use there **(Hermans, 2015)** – which, of course, may not be representative of companies in general, but certainly provides interesting statistics – found that 58% of them contained no formulas at all! In such cases, you could just use Word.

Data analysis

Company systems often have the necessary data, but standard reports cannot always readily answer business questions or are not in the desired structure. Luckily, IT systems often enable data to be exported in Excel-compatible format where they can be further manipulated and analysed as required. For example, for one client I analysed sales delivery data and generated tables and graphs to show lead times and whether deliveries were on time or late e.g., by product category and customer. Such analysis can be performed on a one-off or regular basis. In the latter case, such workbooks can develop into fully-fledged, standalone tools.

Tools

Spreadsheet tools are used regularly for data capture, and/or analysis either on a standalone basis (there is little or no data from outside) or using system reports or data exports as inputs.

For example, I developed an Excel tool for a media client to capture sales data by customer, project, and team, which produced a dashboard and graphs for analysis. Another client manages the renting out of various office buildings on behalf of their clients and uses a number of Excel tools to analyse and control overdue rental payments and to identify and prepare for upcoming rental increases, among other things.

Reporting

Accounting departments often produce regular reports or report collections (usually called packs). A monthly reporting pack typically includes profit and loss accounts ('income statements' in USA and Canada) showing monthly and year-to-date performance and key performance indicators (KPIs). The preparation of such packs is often performed in Excel. Other uses are also possible. For one client, I developed a daily sales report to take a detailed system report as an input and to produce output summaries e.g., by brand and business unit. Such reporting typically compares actual and plan figures and shows the variances which can be used to initiate corrective or supportive action, if necessary. But to do that, you need plan numbers.

Planning

Company systems typically only contain actual data. Plan data, if any, must usually be input from outside the system so you need a separate tool for that. Excel is typically the tool of choice for planning purposes. Examples of planning spreadsheets include sales, personnel costs, complete profit and loss accounts and cash flows.

Financial modelling

In some cases, the scope and functionality of a planning workbook warrants the title of financial model or business model, in the sense that the whole business activity is being modelled. Such models usually include integrated financial statements comprising profit and loss account, balance sheet and cash flow and can depict just a single entity or a whole group of companies. A comprehensive model like this can be used for strategic planning. Such models are necessary in M&A transactions to model the target enterprise, to perform indicative valuations and often to model the required financing. Financial modelling is also used to plan and optimise project financing e.g., for a new building such as an office block or factory, or a new solar park.

So, Excel spreadsheets are everywhere and widely used for all sorts of purposes. From now on, however, we will ignore simple lists and focus on the other uses i.e., spreadsheets that actually do something with numbers, usually with formulas or pivot tables, and which often support key decision making, as the F1F9 survey quoted above shows (F1F9 DD). Spreadsheets are great for these tasks, but without training in best practice techniques, the end results can be hard to understand and use, inflexible and unreliable. Which brings us neatly to the subject of errors.

SPREADSHEET ERRORS ARE COMMON

'Research on spreadsheet errors is substantial, compelling, and unanimous.' (Panko, 2015). In his earlier, perhaps more famous study into spreadsheet errors, Professor Panko reported that studies 'found errors in at least 86% of the spreadsheets audited.' (Panko, Spreadsheet Errors: What We Know. What We Think We Can Do, 2008)

A similar statistic is also quoted by F1F9 in a survey which they carried out: 'It is reported that close to 90% of spreadsheets contain errors and that approximately 50% of spreadsheet models in use operationally in large businesses have material defects.' (F1F9 DD). In a separate report into spreadsheet usage by large businesses in the UK (F1F9 CDS), they found that:

- 17% have suffered financial loss due to poor spreadsheets

- 33% reported poor decision making due to spreadsheet problems

- 57% said bad spreadsheets have caused wasted time

So, errors and problems are common. But why is that? Research has been conducted into how and why errors arise. The key findings are:

- Error rates for simple, individual actions are low, typically between 1% and 5% (Panko, 2014). When developing a spreadsheet, however, many such actions are required, and the overall error rate increases dramatically.

- Errors can be extremely difficult to detect and correct (Panko, 2015).

- Despite the above two facts, spreadsheet developers and users are typically overconfident in their spreadsheets. This is because people are not effective at detecting errors, especially when working alone (Panko, 2015). This finding is also consistent with general research into overconfidence which has, for example, found that 93% of US drivers estimate themselves to be above-average (Dobelli, 2013).

That is the detailed view. Looking at matters from a higher level, the F1F9 report (F1F9 CDS) suggests that a lack of formal training is a key cause. This is a vital point that we address in chapter 1 'Be prepared' and indeed it is the main reason I wrote this book: to train you in best practice techniques. I am also convinced that many spreadsheet developers and users are unaware of the different kinds of errors that arise, and we therefore cover over 20 real-life examples in chapter 3 'Learn from horror stories' to get you 'risk aware', following the proverb 'A danger foreseen is half avoided'.

ERRORS CAN HAVE SERIOUSLY DAMAGING CONSEQUENCES

The F1F9 report (F1F9 CDS) found that spreadsheets are used in the preparation of British company accounts worth up to 1.0 trillion pounds, by UK manufacturers for pricing decisions up to 170 billion pounds worth of business and that spreadsheet analysis underpins up to 38 billion pounds of British private sector investments p.a. With spreadsheets being so widely used for such large amounts, the potential impact of errors can justifiably be described as enormous. And this is not just a theoretical risk, as we will see in numerous examples in chapter 3 'Learn from horror stories'.

Spreadsheet errors are not just limited to data and formula errors, but also include user errors such as data breaches. Data may have been complete and accurate but if they are made available to unauthorised persons, this can also have significant damaging consequences. A study by IBM (IBM, 2020) reports that the global average cost of a data breach is $3.86 million. Data breaches include spreadsheets containing confidential company or personal employee information being inadvertently sent to unauthorised persons and you will see examples of this in chapter 3 'Learn from horror stories'.

These are the kinds of errors all serious users of Excel want to avoid. The million-dollar (sometimes billion dollar) question is how? How can you avoid material errors and create reliable spreadsheets for analysis, reporting, planning and decision making? You will find the answers in this book.

HOW TO EXCEL AT CREATING RELIABLE, USER-FRIENDLY SPREADSHEETS

The Excel 'holy grail' is to create spreadsheets that are reliable, easy to use and flexible. This book will help you achieve that. You will learn how to implement best practice and avoid material errors. You will:

+ learn Golden Ground Rules for working with Excel to improve the flexibility and ease of use of your spreadsheets and minimise the risk of error

+ learn how errors can occur – largely based upon real-life horror stories – and become familiar with techniques to avoid such errors

+ fill your tool bag with 'how2excel' tips to help you in error avoidance and in your spreadsheet work in general

The book is packed with practical examples and screenshots to help you understand and is written is a friendly tone rather than as a dry user manual.

Note: I used a mixture of Excel 2019 and Excel 365 for the screenshots in this book. If you are using another version of Excel, things may look different, and some functionality may have changed.

In **chapter 1 'Be prepared'**, you will learn what to do before starting to develop a spreadsheet and how best to plan your work.

In **chapter 2 'Follow Gary's Golden Ground Rules'**, you will learn all five of my tried and tested Golden Ground Rules for spreadsheet development. Rules 1 to 3 cover clear spreadsheet structure, calculations and design. Rules 4 and 5 explain how to restrict access and changes to your spreadsheets and make it clear for users how to use them. Follow these to help ensure that your spreadsheets are easy to use and to avoid errors.

A key focus in this book is error prevention. Whatever your spreadsheet is intended to do, its results must be reliable. A key concept for developing reliable spreadsheets is error prevention, since 'an ounce of prevention is better than a pound of cure'. The preparation guidance in chapter 1 and my Golden Ground Rules in chapter 2 will help you here. Additionally, you should be aware of how errors arise and how such errors can be avoided.

In **chapter 3 'Learn from horror stories'**, you will therefore learn about more than 20 real-life spreadsheet errors which had significant, damaging consequences – largely financial but also reputational – for the organisations and the people involved. These horror stories are grouped into categories to get you better acquainted with the kinds of errors that occur. In each case, you will learn how such errors arise and practical techniques to avoid them. These are often illustrated with simple Excel examples to help you better understand them. As a bonus, these examples are all available in Excel files that you can download and review to further improve your understanding. Please visit https://www.knott-consulting.com/en/book/ for the download link.

In **chapter 4 'Avoid common function errors'**, you will understand various errors that can arise when using common functions such as VLOOKUP, NPV and IFERROR and how to avoid them.

At this point in the book, we end the focus on error prevention. Two additional steps are needed to weed out any errors which do manage to slip through, and you will learn these in the next two chapters.

In **chapter 5 'Detect errors'**, you will learn how to identify errors, in case prevention fails. You will learn my three-pronged approach to error detection: built-in checks, review and testing by the developer, and independent review and testing.

In **chapter 6 'Find and correct errors',** you will learn how to find and correct errors, including those that you had not previously detected! This is a vital step that should not be underestimated or omitted if you want to be really sure that your spreadsheets are reliable.

Finally, in **chapter 7 'How to excel'**, you will find advice on how best to apply your new-found knowledge and also a useful checklist of all the major concepts from the book for you to use in your Excel work. As a bonus, you can download and printout a PDF of the checklist for easy reference.

Finally, I would like to emphasise that the focus of the book is to teach you how to excel at creating reliable, user-friendly spreadsheets. And that's with whichever version of Excel you are using. Microsoft continues to add new functionality to Excel such as Power Query, Power Pivot and dynamic arrays (functions such as SORT, FILTER and UNIQUE). The advice I give for pivot tables applies equally to power pivot tables. For the rest, my advice is often general enough for you to apply, whichever functions you are using.

Now let's get started...

1. Be prepared

'Let's start at the very beginning, a very good place to start.'
from The Sound of Music by Rogers and Hammerstein

What is 'the very beginning' of a spreadsheet? Well, first you need to decide if you should use a spreadsheet at all.

1.1. DECIDE IF A SPREADSHEET IS THE BEST SOLUTION

As you now know, I am a great fan of Excel, but it may not always be the best solution for your task. As a rule, standard software and reports are formally tested by the developer before release and by each company upon implementation, so these may represent readily accessible and reliable sources of data. So, ask yourself the following questions before you fire up Excel.

- What do you need to process, calculate, analyse or report?

- Does an existing system or data warehouse provide the necessary functionality? If so, why not use that? If not, could an IT request to get a new report be a sensible option, especially if the report will be needed on a regular basis? For example, to produce a new report of sales by invoice date instead of by order date could represent a simple change to an existing report.

- Is an off-the-shelf software solution available which can meet most or all your requirements, for example, for project planning or recording sales made? This may be easier and cheaper to implement, use and maintain.

If you finally decide that a spreadsheet is the best tool for the job, then you are in luck, because Excel is very flexible and you can get historical (actual) data in Excel-format from most systems for analysis, reporting or as a basis for planning. But in order to create understandable, reliable spreadsheets, you need to know what you are doing, especially to avoid errors.

1.2. GET TRAINED

Excel does not make errors!

Users make errors. In fact, *to err is human.*

One report into spreadsheet use (F1F9 CDS) found that a third of the financial decision-makers using spreadsheets in large UK firms are given no formal Excel training. That is like driving a car without having had any lessons: accidents are just waiting to happen. And that is bad enough when an Excel user is putting together a small analysis e.g., of overdue accounts. But if the Excel user is developing a valuation model for a large company with multiple business areas, mistakes are more likely and can be much larger in both size and effect.

Therefore, it is essential that developers of Excel spreadsheets should be appropriately trained. And not just in Excel but also in business fundamentals as well as accounting essentials and financing, where relevant. To continue the car driving analogy, that is like a car driver being able to mechanically drive a car.

But to really avoid accidents, a driver also needs higher-level skills: to be aware of risks and to amend their driving style to match the situation on the road. Car insurance companies offer discounts to drivers who have passed an advanced driving test: the reason is obvious... such drivers have fewer accidents. So where can you get your 'advanced Excel driving lessons'? This book will help you here by giving you a best practice approach to prevent, detect and correct errors. On top of that, you will learn valuable tricks and tips to help you develop reliable spreadsheets and avoid errors.

If you are a CFO or manager wondering if it is worth getting your staff properly trained in Excel, then think about these short questions:

1. Be prepared

'What if we train our staff and they leave?'

'What if we don't train them and they stay... and make Excel errors?'

If you think Excel errors aren't that serious, then please go directly to chapter 3 'Learn from horror stories', where you will learn about Excel horror stories and the large financial and reputational losses that have occurred as the result of spreadsheet errors.

1.3. PLAN YOUR SPREADSHEET

'If you are failing to plan, you are planning to fail.'
Alan Lakein, American author on planning
and time management

Planning is an extremely valuable activity that brings many benefits. According to Brian Tracy, for every minute you spend planning, you can save up to ten minutes in execution (Tracy, 2014). So, twelve minutes of planning can save you up to two hours of work! On top of that efficiency bonus, you are also likely to make fewer errors, because you have a clearer idea about what you are trying to achieve and what you need to do to meet that goal. To return to the driving analogy: it is better to plan out your route in advance, especially for a long journey. Without advance planning, the route you take may well not be the best, you may waste time and resources, and you may even get lost and arrive late at your destination – or not at all. Here, the compass is more important than the clock: there is no point steaming ahead if you are heading in the wrong direction. So please follow the key planning points outlined below.

Be clear on spreadsheet purpose and scope

That's not what I wanted,' wails the user on seeing the first draft of the model.

'But I assumed that's what you wanted!' replies the developer.

Assumption is the mother of all disasters. The rule here is: do not assume… that just makes an ASS of U and ME! Instead, discuss and agree up front, ideally in written form.

Note: Here I am talking about assumptions in your head e.g., about what the user wants or what key values should be calculated. Such assumptions are bad. By contrast, assumptions about the future such as sales prices, personnel requirements or interest rates are often necessary. These are fine as long as they are explicitly and clearly depicted as inputs in the model and not hard-coded in formulas.

If the spreadsheet is to be used for an important task or decision, and especially if it is expected to have some degree of complexity, it is a good idea to get together with key model users or sponsors to discuss these topics in advance so that everyone agrees what the **spreadsheet purpose** is as well as what the key outputs should be and what key functionality it should have.

The model purpose must be at the heart of everything you include in the model. If an input, a calculation, or an output does not support the purpose, then leave it out. That saves both time and complexity and reduces the risk of error, including the worst error of all… the model is not fit for purpose!

What is the **spreadsheet scope**? For example, in a financial model, what legal entities or business divisions should be included? And at what level of detail, for example, should sales be planned? In total, or by region, or brand or at stock-keeping-unit level? If this is not clearly agreed up front, it is all too easy to get it wrong which can also result in the spreadsheet being not fit for purpose.

Consider your spreadsheet users

It is very important to consider your users:

- Who are they?

- Which of them will be the **key users**?

- What is their level of Excel skills and knowledge?

You should strive to make all your spreadsheets easy to use and understand. Knowing your users can help you design and develop the model accordingly and so avoid errors in usage. For even if a completed spreadsheet is both theoretically and technically perfect, please remember:

'A fool with a tool is still a fool... and a dangerous one.'

So, thinking about users early on is paramount to creating spreadsheets that are not only reliable in form but also reliable in use.

Select an appropriate language

Especially for English speaking users this is perhaps a 'no brainer', but for non-English speaking countries you should consider the end-users and what language will be most appropriate for text in the spreadsheet: data labels, instructions, comments on data sources etc. In the world of corporate finance, financial models are often developed in English because this allows a greater number of potential company purchasers or financiers to use model outputs. If model users are not proficient enough in the language used, however, they may well make errors in using the model, so think about this and agree on the language to be used in advance. In some cases, it may be appropriate to include two languages: for the data labels, typically in column A, insert an extra column for the labels in the second language. Instructions and cover sheets can be simply duplicated in their entirety and translated. I heartily recommend https://www.deepl.com/ for such work: the quality of translations is high, thanks to artificial intelligence, and you can copy a whole column of labels into deepl and get back the whole column translated for pasting into your spreadsheet. For a fee, pro users can create custom dictionaries to further improve the quality of translations.

Select an appropriate currency and units

Decide at the model planning and design stage which currency (if appropriate) and units you will generally use in your spreadsheet. I call the chosen currency the 'reporting currency' of the spreadsheet and any values in other currencies must be converted before use. The best units to choose depends upon the size of the numbers which you will be dealing with: the larger the numbers, the less digits you should show. For monetary units, I generally recommend either:

- Thousands of Dollars/Pounds/Euros/etc. (with no decimal places) or

- Millions of Dollars/Pounds/Euros/etc. (with one decimal place)

The key here is to (i) avoid inconsistencies which could cause errors and (ii) restrict the length of numbers to make them easier to enter, use and interpret.

Consider time, budget and data available

These are key factors to be clear on early in the planning process as they will limit, to a greater or lesser extent, what can realistically be achieved to meet the spreadsheet purpose and scope. The risk of error typically rises when working under time, cost or scope pressure e.g., to meet unrealistic expectations of developing an all-singing, all-dancing model in just a few days. The best approach here may well be to start small and add detail and functionality to the spreadsheet over time, provided time and resources (budget and people) continue to be available. This approach has the big advantage that a working version of the spreadsheet can be quickly made available to support early decision making. It may also help to determine priorities for further development of the spreadsheet but be aware here of 'scope creep', which may result in requests from the users e.g., for additional functionality which lie outside the original scope. In such cases, you may have to reject such requests in order to remain within time and budget constraints. On the other hand, such requests can be for great, new functionality that strongly support the model purpose. In such cases, it may be sensible

1. Be prepared

to revise the originally agreed scope and, for larger spreadsheets, to get this agreed with project sponsors or users. Any budget and timescale effects should also be considered here and similarly approved.

The detail or functionality of some spreadsheets may have to be limited if input data is not available in the required level of detail or reliability. For example, this can be an issue when developing a model of a company to be purchased where the amount of data available may well be limited in the early stages of an M&A transaction or if customised reports need to be developed to extract necessary information from relevant IT systems.

Define key content

> ***'Begin with the end in mind.'***
> *Stephen Covey, author of The 7 Habits of*
> *Highly Effective People*

When planning your spreadsheet, you should follow Covey's advice: start with the desired outputs and work backwards. This helps ensure that you have everything you need in your model, and nothing is unnecessary. If you go in the other direction, from inputs to outputs, this is not ensured. Unnecessary inputs and calculations may be included, and the end result may not meet requirements, because they are based upon what is available rather than what is needed to meet the spreadsheet purpose.

Content should be split into inputs, calculations and outputs. This helps ensure clarity in the model structure and data flow. It helps not only you during development but also the users who will be less familiar with the spreadsheet than you. Everyone then knows where to go to update the inputs, amend or understand the calculations or review the outputs.

Outputs: What outputs are necessary to meet the purpose and scope?

For example: your aim is to perform an analysis of gross profits by business area – equipment sales, spares sales and servicing. Planned outputs are the actual gross profit, both as a monetary value and expressed as a percentage of sales, by business area and year.

Calculations: What calculations are necessary to produce these outputs?

What level of detail is required?

Continuing our example: calculations would be needed for (i) net sales = gross sales less sales discounts and rebates given and (ii) cost of goods sold which could be the sum of direct material, labour and other production costs for manufacturers or simply purchase costs for distributors. If shipping costs are also included, calculations may be necessary to apportion total shipping costs to business areas using a suitable distribution key, say in proportion to sales.

Inputs: What data are necessary and available? What assumptions (inputs) must be made e.g., sales prices, cost inflation, tax rates?

Who can provide these and when?

Completing our example: inputs would typically include detailed sales data at invoice or product level. You need gross sales data as well as sales discounts (deducted from invoice amount), rebates (such as volume rebates, deducted later) as well as costs of goods sold along with the business area in each case. If appropriate, you could also take shipping costs into account. Here it may be necessary to apportion such costs to the three business areas (equipment, spares and servicing) using an assumption e.g., in proportion to gross sales. The business area 'servicing' may be exempted here if service personnel take their own parts for servicing with them. All things to think about!

Once you have your design, you can start work on development. Here you should work in the 'natural order' of inputs, then calculations and finally outputs. This ensures that when you develop your calculations, you can link them to your inputs, because these are already available. Similarly, when you develop the outputs, you can link them to the calculations as these are already there.

Define key functionality

What should the spreadsheet be able to do above and beyond the purpose and content already discussed? For example, in planning models it is often desired to depict several scenarios, typically base, best, and worst cases. If so, this is vital to know before starting development work as it critically affects model structure and complexity and requires inputs for each scenario. Sometimes, users want an all-singing, all-dancing spreadsheet. This is usually not desirable as it can make the spreadsheet overly complex and can exceed time and cost budgets. As already mentioned, the best approach in such cases can be to start small and add detail and functionality to the spreadsheet over time. This approach has the great advantage that a complete model – with inputs, calculations and outputs – can be produced efficiently to help guide early decision making. The risk of error is lower, and testing is also easier because the model is simpler.

Define an appropriate period structure

Time periods are often needed. If so, these should also be agreed in the planning phase.

Length: How long should they be? Annual and monthly periods are common. In many cases, I find annual periods are best as you generally do not need too many and so you have a better overview of each sheet's content including results. A monthly period structure may be necessary however e.g., for company restructuring or detailed cash flow models, where you need to know if you can survive each and every individual month and what the financing needs in each month are expected to be. Project planning models are also often depicted with monthly periods, at least to start with, where it is important to plan and control the timing of large investment and financing cash flows in the early stages. In such cases, I usually also present annual figures but keep these separate to the monthly columns, so that formulas are consistent within each block (monthly figures or annual figures), which reduces the risk of error.

Number: For data analysis, what period should be analysed, e.g., last year and current year-to-date? For planning models, how many actual and plan periods should be depicted, e.g., two actual and five plan years?

Direction: I recommend depicting periods across the spreadsheet page and content (sales, cost of sales etc.) down the page. One reason is that this is what people are used to, e.g., from annual accounts. It also reflects the common layout of graphs which have time on the x-axis. If you have annual and monthly periods, I generally recommend that you start with annual periods on the left (these give an overview to start with) followed by the monthly periods on the right (which are used to generate the annual figures). This does not conform with the general best practice rule of calculating from left to right and from top to bottom. However, there is a good reason for doing this – the important annual numbers come first – so it is an acceptable exception.

I recommend you put a blank column (of width 2) between the annual and monthly blocks to create an optical break between the two and to reduce the risk of copying an annual period formula into the months or vice versa.

Planning these key spreadsheet elements in advance helps focus attention and provide clarity on what is needed in terms of data inputs and model content, structure and functionality. And this, in turn, helps improve reliability by reducing errors in both the development and usage phases. For example, if you do not adequately plan your spreadsheet, you may need to radically redesign it if it later becomes clear that it does not meet the stated purpose. This is perhaps the worst error of all!

Alternatively, it could be that your model is 'technically perfect' but reliable data at the relevant level of detail is not available. Without suitable input data, your model is like a car without fuel and cannot help the user get to their desired destination.

Document your design

Last but by no means least! You should document the above planning components (the 'model design') in an appropriate level of detail, at least for important and larger scope models. Focus on key model content and functionality, as covered in the preceding sections. Send this model design document to key users and ideally get them to approve it before you start.

1.4. BEST PRACTICE CHECKLIST

- Decide if a spreadsheet is the best solution

- Get trained

- Plan your spreadsheet and consider:

    - Purpose and scope

    - Users

    - Language

    - Reporting currency and units

    - Time, budget and data available

    - Content and functionality

    - Period structure

- Document your design

2. Follow Gary's Golden Ground Rules

'Imitate nothing except principle.'
Frank Lloyd Wright, American architect

Golden Ground Rules – who needs them?

We all do! Spreadsheets should be reliable, understandable and easy to use. These are three qualities you must strive for, and they are interrelated. But if you had a spreadsheet that could only have one of these qualities, which would you choose? I think it is obvious: reliability is king. Put another way: what good is a spreadsheet which is understandable and easy to use but not reliable? Answer: no good!

So, what makes a spreadsheet reliable? Well, its inputs, calculations and outputs must be free of material error. But that is not enough because someone has to use it and they can make errors even when there were technically none in the spreadsheet inputs, calculations and outputs. To avoid user error a spreadsheet, therefore, also needs to be understandable and easy to use.

With errors, you can either prevent them or you can detect and correct them. Obviously, prevention is much better than cure. If you can prevent errors then you save yourself time and cost later in searching for and removing them. In the worst case, an error goes undetected and uncorrected and causes a material error in decision making with serious consequences.

There is a Japanese concept for error prevention, originally developed by Toyota, called *poka-yoke*, which means 'mistake-proofing' or 'inadvertent error prevention'. The idea is to build error prevention into a process such as car manufacture. But the concept can also be applied to spreadsheets, for example through the use of data validation for inputs (like drop-down lists) to restrict data input to only valid entries, a topic we cover under Golden Ground Rule #4.

Error prevention can best be achieved by following my Golden Ground Rules during spreadsheet development and amendment. I compiled these over the years from a combination of rules I have read and other that I have developed from personal experience, and I have grouped them under five headings for easier consumption.

The benefits of Gary's Golden Ground Rules

My Golden Ground Rules for spreadsheet development bring important benefits:

- Spreadsheet development is more **efficient**.

- The **ease of use** and **flexibility** of the spreadsheet are increased.

- The risk of error is minimised, hence results are more reliable.

The rules cover five key spreadsheet areas and are as follows:

1. **Use a clear, logical workbook structure**

   Decide what worksheets you need, get them in order and give them clear names.

2. **Keep your worksheets as clear and simple as possible**

   Ensure each worksheet is clearly laid out and easy to use.

3. **Use a clear, clean, consistent design**

   Ensure the whole workbook has a clear, professional look and feel.

4. **Restrict access, inputs and changes**

   Ensure that only authorised users can access and change your spreadsheet.

5. **Write instructions for users**

   Ensure that users know what to do and in what order.

Let's now go through these in detail in the following five sub-chapters.

2.1. RULE #1 – USE A CLEAR, LOGICAL WORKBOOK STRUCTURE

Decide what worksheets you need, get them in order and give them clear names.

WORKBOOK STRUCTURE

Having planned your model, you should have a clear idea about what content you need. This should be distributed sensibly over multiple worksheets. Inputs, calculations and outputs should be separated as far as possible. For larger models, each depicted entity or region may require its own set of such sheets.

Data should clearly flow in one direction: input sheets feed the calculation sheets which produce results for the output sheets. If your spreadsheet includes multiple 'units', such as legal entities, geographical or business areas, then this logic should be followed for each unit depicted. Ensure that the order of the sheets in the spreadsheet reflects this data flow. Typically, the order used is either input sheets on the left to output sheets on the right or the other way around:

- **Left to right:** great for spreadsheets which need to be regularly updated. You can then work through the sheets in a logical order: first update the inputs (left-hand tabs), then review the calculations and maybe update any assumptions there, then analyse the outputs (right-hand tabs).

- **Right to left:** great for spreadsheets where the key user is a manager whose focus is the outputs for decision making. In this case, values flow from inputs at the back of the spreadsheet (right-hand tabs, which the key user will rarely, if ever, look at) via calculations in the middle to the outputs at the front (left-hand tabs) where the 'important stuff' is.

If you need to reorder one or more worksheets, you can drag and drop them using their name tabs or, if your spreadsheet has a lot of worksheets, it may be more efficient to right-click on the tab name and select 'Move or copy'. You can also select multiple sheet tabs and move them all at once using either method.

 **how2excel tip**

Use separator tabs for each new section

Using separator tabs makes the model structure clearer for both developer and user. A separator tab is simply an (almost) empty worksheet with just the name of the section followed by a space and a greater than symbol, such as 'Inputs >'. The greater than symbol represents an arrow that points to the worksheets that follow. On the separator tab itself, you can include the worksheet name (say in cell A1) in a larger font size and in cell A3 the explanatory text: 'This is a separator sheet.'

The workbook structure also depends on the purpose of your spreadsheet or model.

- **Data analysis and spreadsheet tools:** I usually have sections for inputs, calculations and outputs plus a general section for instructions, checks and a change log (see below).

- **Financial planning models:** I usually have sections for each depicted entity, which then contains worksheets for inputs, calculations and outputs for that entity. I also have a general section for instructions, checks and a change log.

 **how2excel tip**

Make back-ups regularly and before major changes

Before you make any major change in a model, but especially to the structure, always create a **back-up** of the model before you start (i) in case in case things go wrong and you need to revert to the old version and (ii) so you can compare the new and old versions if you want to better understand the effects of the change or to check that there were none, if that should be the case.

If you autosave your files in OneDrive, you should be able to review version history of a selected file and open older version(s), if required.

SHEET NAMES

Give your sheets clear, meaningful names. Excel limits you to 31 characters in tab names but that is probably too many to use in most cases. Longer names *may* be more meaningful but can lead to long formulas when such sheets are linked to and you can only see a few sheet names at the bottom of your screen, which can hamper effective navigation. On the other hand, sheet names that are too short and contain cryptic abbreviations may be incomprehensible. Similar considerations apply to other content such as column headings. A Dilbert cartoon makes the point well: a spreadsheet developer is irritated that Dilbert has failed to understand what a particular column is for. 'This column is the ratio of product returns to gross revenue excluding sales taxes, annualised. It's clearly labelled "ROPRTGRESTA".'

You may use abbreviations such as 'FinStats' for financial statements or entity or country identifiers such as 'DE' for Germany, but please provide a list or explanations e.g., on the cover sheet.

As so often in life, the trick is to find the right balance. You should also try to be consistent as this makes it easier to understand and use your spreadsheet. For example, if you have multiple regions in your model, you may group the sheets for each region together and start each sheet name with an abbreviation of the region: EUR for Europe, US for America and so on. For countries, I tend to use the ISO two-letter or three-letter abbreviations.

Let us now take a look at some key sheets which you should include in all but the simplest of workbooks.

COVER SHEET

'Read all about it…' – the cover sheet gives someone opening the spreadsheet a summary of key information and could look like this.

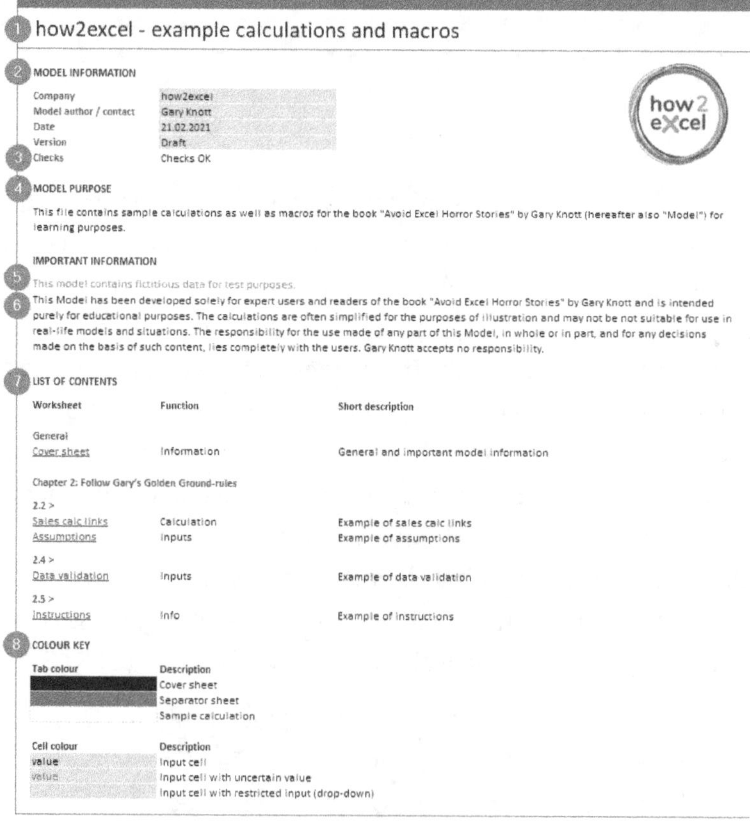

Include the cover sheet at the front (tab at the left-hand end) of the workbook in order to give key information including the purpose and content to anyone using the file. It should include:

1. Name of the spreadsheet giving a brief idea of its purpose.

2. Model information: company, model author or contact, model date and version (e.g., 'Draft', 'Version 1' or 'Updated per key user meeting 24th June 20xx').

3. Result of checks within the workbook (see sub-chapter 5.1 'Build in error checks and a master check').

4. Model purpose: a brief but informative statement of what the spreadsheet is intended to do.

5. Significant model simplifications, restrictions or currently missing data or functionality, if any, should be mentioned, e.g., 'this model currently contains fictitious data for test purposes' or 'tax loss carry-forwards are currently not depicted'.

6. Important information including who the spreadsheet is for and any restrictions on use. e.g., 'This model has been developed for expert users in the finance department of company XYZ. It represents an unaudited draft and is to be handled in strict confidence. It may not be passed in whole or in part to any third party without prior written agreement.'

   Note: As we will cover in chapter 5 'Detect errors', a spreadsheet should be reviewed and tested but, as a rule, is never 'audited'.

7. List of contents: a list of sheet names (ideally with hyperlinks), function (e.g., information, checks, inputs, calculations, planning, outputs) and a short description such as 'Actual P&L and balance sheet data'.

   Note: P&L = Profit and Loss account, often called an Income Statement in America and Canada.

8. Colour key for sheet tabs and cells: please do not use more than (say) five colours and these should not be too bright. I find bright

yellow the worst – it hurts the eyes to look at blocks of such cells. If you use lots of colours, especially bright colours, these can make a model look garish and unprofessional and can reduce rather than increase user-friendliness and so increase the risk of error.

If important data is provisional or significant functionality is missing, include a very clear comment e.g., in red on the cover sheet to make matter clear, for example 'This model currently contains some fictional data for test purposes' or 'This model does not yet incorporate a scenario for increased production capacity'. In such cases, it is perhaps wise to also add a comment similar to 'This version of the model is therefore not suitable for decision-making purposes'. This should make matters clear and help avoid errors in usage.

Select the cover sheet before you save your file. The spreadsheet then opens on that sheet when a user opens the file so he or she can immediately see key information including version and purpose. That is helpful and looks professional.

DASHBOARD / COCKPIT

In large or complex spreadsheets, it is often useful to have a dashboard sheet towards the front of the model with key results in graphs and tables to facilitate an analysis of the results. If you have key assumptions or scenario switches, these can be included so that the user can change these and immediately see the impact of changes made on results. Such a sheet is then often called a cockpit because it contains both key inputs and key results. This is a key worksheet and offers significant benefits:

- **Facilitates control of the model:** key inputs, assumptions and switches (e.g., for scenarios) can be grouped together here and easily reviewed or amended.

- **Enables efficient evaluation of results:** tables and graphs of key outputs and KPIs clearly show the effects of key inputs and scenario settings.

- **Clarity:** the user knows where to go to perform these tasks. In some models I have seen, such functionality is either not available or is hard to find.

INSTRUCTIONS AND CHECKS

These two sheets are so important that they get their own explanations later in the book: instructions are covered under Golden Ground Rule #5 and checks are covered in chapter 5 'Detect errors'.

CHANGE LOG

Consider including a list of the major model changes, perhaps at the end (worksheet tab at the right-hand end) of the model. This gives both model developers and users clarity about what changes have been made and when. I do not include every change here, especially not every input change, only those with a significant (or potentially significant) impact on results or functionality.

I typically include the following columns on this sheet:

- Date
- Model version (what have you written in the 'version' cell on the cover sheet after you made the change?)
- Name of changer
- Sheet name(s)
- Details – a brief description of what was changed and maybe also why (no novels here please, it is just a change log)

2.2. RULE #2 – KEEP YOUR WORKSHEETS AS CLEAR AND SIMPLE AS POSSIBLE

Analogous to Golden Ground Rule #1 – use a clear, logical workbook structure, you should also keep each worksheet as clear as possible by using a logical, consistent structure within each worksheet and by keeping content, especially calculations, as simple as possible.

Consistency is key for spreadsheet construction and helps make them understandable and easy to use which, in turn, reduces both developer and user error and improves reliability. It follows one of the four principles of good design: repetition. More details follow in Golden Ground Rule #3 below.

In the context of spreadsheet design, repeated blocks of calculations within a sheet or across several sheets help both spreadsheet developers (develop and test once, use many times) and users (understand one, understand all).

As in other areas of work, it is also more enjoyable to use a tidy, professional-looking work area, such as a well-built spreadsheet. That is why one client came to me with a spreadsheet she had developed and asked me to make it 'look good'. To do that, I used some of the tips that follow.

We will cover columns first, then rows, formulas and finally whole sheets.

COLUMNS

Use columns consistently in all sheets

Column A is usually reserved for labels, such as 'Sales'. Column B can be used for constants (period-independent data) such as units e.g., EUR for euros, TEUR or k EUR for thousands of euros. Periods, such as years or months, and period-specific data, such as sales per year, start in column C. Once defined, these column usages should be consistently applied on all sheets so that formulas containing links to other sheets remain correct if copied to the right.

I generally define the column headers on one sheet called 'Settings' and link to these on all other sheets. This is especially useful if a workbook has to be regularly updated with actual data. You can set the last actual period here; this then automatically updates the period type in the column headers (Actual or Plan), which then flow through the whole model. Formulas on other sheets can then use these headers in calculations – in actuals periods the actual (input) value is used, otherwise the plan value is used, and the relevant value flows further in the model.

Obvious exceptions to this rule are sheets without model data such as the cover sheet and instructions.

Use consistent column widths

I generally use a width of 12. This means that 12 digits without 1000 separators or decimal points will fit into the cell. The same cannot be said of letters because most fonts nowadays are not mono-spaced (equal width), so you may well get more than 12 letters or text characters in the cell. This should be wide enough for most purposes. If you find this is too narrow, and your numbers do not fit, then you are probably using numbers that have too many digits and this makes the model harder to use and interpret. Consider changing the default unit displayed in your spreadsheet from say, US dollars to thousands or even millions of US dollars, perhaps with a single decimal place.

If the data are small numbers or otherwise restricted in length (e.g., short account numbers) I sometimes use a column width of 8 or 10. I make empty separator columns, between say, annual and monthly columns, a width of 2. That is wide enough to make a clear optical break but not so wide that it takes up unnecessary screen space which limits the amount you can see on your screen without scrolling.

Align your column data

This point addresses the third design concept: alignment. My preferred solution depends upon the type of data in each column. Whatever you choose, please format the column headers the same as the data in the column (left, centre or right).

- Text – either (i) use the standard setting, which is aligned left – this is best for longer data entries such as product descriptions or comments but is also suitable for shorter entries or (ii) align centre – this can be good for shorter data entries such as invoice or account number.

- Numbers (including currency and percentages) – use the standard setting, which is aligned right. Please do not align to centre or left(!) as I have sometimes seen in newspaper tables, for example, as it is then harder to scan for larger numbers and do mental arithmetic. The standard setting also has the advantage that if any numbers are formatted as text, these will be automatically left-aligned, and you can easily spot them and correct them. We cover this in detail in a horror story in sub-chapter 3.2 'Incorrect inputs'.

- Dates – dates are just numbers, really (the number of days since 1st January 1900, formatted so it looks like a date) so you can follow the advice on numbers. Alternatively, align centre, since dates are short and the same length, so they are easy enough to scan.

Sort your columns

If you have many columns, decide which of them are more important than the others and make these more accessible by placing them to the left (on all sheets, of course!) With annual and monthly periods, for example, annual figures are generally more important and give a better overview than the monthly figures. Place the annual columns to the left, followed by a narrow blank column (with a width of 2) and then the monthly columns.

For data analysis, you have more flexibility to sort the columns. This is especially important if there are many of them, so that the most import columns are next to or near the descriptions (often column A or B).

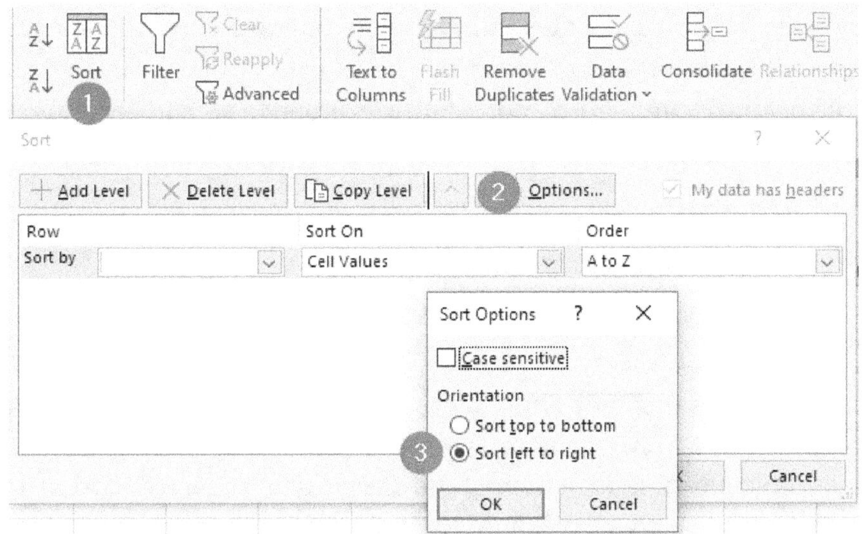

You can sort from left to right in Excel by selecting Sort, Options, Sort left to right.

Use column groupings

If you have many columns in your worksheet, you may also group columns to make it easier to navigate and use. A typical example here is monthly columns covering multiple years. In such cases, I group all but the last month in each year so a user can easily identify and open up a single year to see the months, as necessary. Users can then focus on the full year total columns (to the left) and only open up the monthly columns, as necessary. Please do not mix monthly and annual columns in one block as this increases the risk of copying monthly formulas into the annual columns.

ROWS

Use consistent row heights

I typically use a height of 15 for rows with data and a height of 8 for blank rows before sums or between titles and data. This follows another of the four principles of good design: proximity. Things that belong together (in this case a title and the related data) should be near each other. This not only looks good but helps users to instinctively know what belongs together, so improving user-friendliness and reducing the risk of user error.

Note: Please see sub-chapter 2.3 'Rule #3 – Use a clear, clean, consistent design' for more details of all four principles.

Use blocks

First split the content into logical blocks e.g., split the financial statements into P&L, balance sheet and cash flow. Give each block a clear, bold heading in a consistent design and separate it from the previous block with a blank line. The bold heading represents contrast, another of the four design concepts I mentioned before. It helps both you and your spreadsheet users clearly identify the start of each block and also says what it is for. The blank line is a common design concept known as white space, which agreeably separates the elements on the worksheet. In fact, you may be surprised to learn that typically more than half the cells in a spreadsheet are empty.

Use row groupings

	A
1	**Project Beta**
2	Fin stats - Management Case
3	TEUR
4	Checks OK
5	
6	**Profit & Loss Account**
21	
22	**Balance Sheet**
45	
46	**Cashflow Statement**
76	

I usually group the rows under each heading to facilitate user navigation. This is also useful when developing the model: you can develop one block at a time, in a logical order. When you have finished a block, e.g., values drivers for the P&L, you can close that group of rows and more easily focus on the next block.

Use a clear, consistent structure within each block

I typically use the order: inputs (if appropriate, linked to source worksheets), calculations and results. In simple examples, the calculation is the result, so we have just input and result. The result can then be linked to in the next part of the model, such as financial statements.

	A	B	C	D	E	F
1	SALES (TEUR)	Units	Year 1	Year 2	Year 3	[Cell] Formula
2						
3	Method 1					
4	Sales	TEUR	1,000	1,061	1,125	[C4] =Assumptions!C3*Assumptions!C4/1000
5						
6	Method 2					
7	Sales price per unit	EUR	100	104	108	[C7] =Assumptions!C3
8	Quantity sold	Units	10,000	10,200	10,404	[C8] =Assumptions!C4
9	Sales	TEUR	1,000	1,061	1,125	[C9] =C7*C8/1000

Let's compare and contrast two methods of calculation set-up, shown in the screenshot above. This shows a sales calculation for three years. In each case, the simple logic is the same: sales = units * price but the two methods show how you can make this calculation hard or easy to understand.

Method 1

This is something I have seen a lot in other people's models: a formula is linked to other worksheets or distant parts of the same worksheet. In this example, sales are calculated as sales price per unit (linked to the assumptions worksheet) multiplied with quantity (linked to another part of the assumptions worksheet). This is difficult to understand and review since you have to repeatedly look at another sheet to check what each part of the formula represents.

Method 2

A much better approach is to have a line for each item of data we need – in this case, one line for prices and another line for units, each clearly labelled. These rows are linked to the source worksheet. Then the sales formula is simply price multiplied with units, both of which appear in the lines above. This is much easier to understand, even in this simple example. If the calculation is more complicated, method 2 wins hands down every time. Yes, it makes the calculation longer, but comprehensibility is more important, a point I emphasise again below. And Excel does not charge you by the row, although it admittedly makes the file a little larger.

Sort your data

This final 'row' tip concerns user-friendliness, which also helps reduce the risk of user error, and relates to tables of data e.g., in data analysis spreadsheets.

Do not just leave data in the order you got it, or in alphabetical order. Did you ever see a sports results table like that? Sort the list so the biggest, the best or the oldest items are at the top.

Sorting not only makes it easy for users to focus on the important entries and to compare them, e.g., 'What is the gap between first and second place?' It also helps you to spot errors, e.g., 'That can't be right, let's take a look!'

FORMULAS

Ensure calculations flow from left to right and from top to bottom

---

It is generally accepted best practice to calculate values from left to right and from top to bottom. This is the way we read and so it makes sense for spreadsheets. As an example, let us take sales values. First you can calculate sales units per period e.g., based upon the prior period figure plus a percentage change (calculations flow from left to right by period). Below that, you calculate sales price per period in a similar way with sales prices increasing each year. Finally, below that, you can calculate the sales value (= units * price) per period. Everything is logically arranged and there is no need to follow calculation chains which jump around a whole sheet or (worst still) around the whole workbook.

Exceptions can be justifiable e.g., to put important results on the left where they are easier to read. An example here could be to show annual figures on the left, which are the sum of the monthly figures shown to the right (i.e., a calculation flow from right to left). Another good example is sports' league tables. For each team listed, the number of points is the most important figure, so to show this column first would make reading and interpreting the table easier: the reader's eye does not have to keep scanning between team names on the left and points scores on the right. Here again, the calculation flow is from the right (number of games won and drawn) to the left (points total). These exceptions are justifiable for ease of use and the flow is still logical and understandable.

Use consistent formulas

The Golden Rule here is 'one row, one formula', i.e., all formulas in a row should be the same, copied from left to right. This improves understanding and reduces the risk of error. To do this it may be necessary to use an IF test to see which of two possibilities is appropriate e.g.:

> *=IF(period header = "Actual", cell with actual value, otherwise cell with plan value)*

Such formulas can get long and complicated. If so, do you have to stick with the one formula per row Golden Rule? The short answer is no. The Golden Ground Rules are not immutable laws but rather guidelines. You can break them, but you should only do so knowingly and for a good reason. I sometimes (knowingly) use an inconsistent formula to start a row if this reduces the complexity of the formula (good reason) but in such cases I mark the cell using a special cell format called 'unique formula' for which I use a pale blue background and which I include in the colour key on the cover sheet (see Rule #1 – Use a clear, logical workbook structure). This marks the inconsistency optically and should reduce the risk of errors when copying and pasting formulas... aha, you should say, I need to take care here because that (light blue) formula is different to the neighbouring cells.

Once a calculation has been developed and tested for (say) one business area (e.g., sales calculation), it can be copied and used for other business areas: this is extremely efficient for both the model developer and also for the user: once they understand one calculation logic, they understand them all!

Avoid complexity where possible

This concept has essentially been proposed in various forms by a 14th century philosopher, Albert Einstein (maybe) and also in modern computer science! Let's take a closer look.

The 14th century philosopher was William of Ockham, and he is attributed with the concept of Ockham's razor, which is also known as the law of parsimony. This essentially states that simpler solutions are more likely to be correct than complex ones. When presented with competing hypotheses to solve a problem, one should select the solution with the fewest assumptions. Sounds good for modern spreadsheet calculations, too.

Albert Einstein allegedly said, 'Make everything as simple as possible, but not simpler.' Although there is some doubt about whether he actually said this, the concept stands true, also for spreadsheets.

And last but not least, computer science gives us the concept known as overfitting. You may be able to make a calculation complex enough to very accurately calculate historical results based upon historical input data, but this may be a poor logic to use for the future because it does not reflect random variations, and factors often change over time. So do not go overboard trying to make calculations extremely accurate.

You should apply these concepts to your spreadsheets to keep them as understandable as possible and to reduce the risk of error. Especially if you are calculating plan figures, please remember that these are only an approximation of reality and even the 'most accurate' models will not be 100% correct in predicting future outcomes. Therefore, it may make sense to sacrifice some 'accuracy' and complexity for simplicity... approximately right can be better than 100% wrong.

For example, in a planning model, you want to calculate the cost of goods sold (COGS) over the next five years. Consider two possible approaches:

Method 1

You could split the COGS into component parts: raw materials, production labour and overheads such as rent and electricity. You could then seek to understand the calculation logic of each and get historic values and estimate annual price rises in each case. Then you could use all this information to calculate in detail the planned cost of each component and then add these up to arrive at your planned COGS for the next five years.

Method 2

Alternatively, you could use a single assumption of the COGS as a percentage of sales and consider how this might change over the next five years by speaking to suitably experienced people. This is obviously a much simpler approach, and it may even be a better predictor of future costs. Certainly, it will be easier to model, to understand and to update, e.g., to depict alternative scenarios.

So just because method 1 is possible, it does not necessarily mean you should choose it. Stop and think first. Also consider time and budget available. And remember you can always add more detail later, if necessary. Finally, remember to make your assumptions (e.g., percentage of sales figures) clear by showing them as input cells and note the source of these values possibly in an extra column to the right or in a cell note or comment e.g., '21.2.20xx Discussion with Simon Smith, head of production'. Any notable changes should be explicitly commented on, so it is clear why assumptions are increasing or decreasing significantly e.g., new supplier contract comes into force with higher volume discounts.

Write simple formulas

Once you have decided upon your calculation approach, you should also avoid complexity at the formula level. Here, the KISS principle of 'keep it short and simple' is highly recommended. It makes calculations easier to understand and reduces the risk of errors.

- **Rule of thumb:** The length of a formula in the 'command line' should ideally not exceed the length of your thumb and in any case be no longer than a single line; if necessary, split the calculation across multiple Excel rows and always label rows clearly. This makes the calculation clearer for both developer and users and so reduces the risk or error.

- **Avoid macros for calculations:** For many users, macros represent a 'black box' where the content is not easily accessible. They are usually unnecessary for calculations anyway, since Excel provides numerous functions and great flexibility.

- **Avoid so-called volatile functions like INDIRECT and OFFSET:** Formulas using such functions can be error-prone and make models difficult to understand.

Follow formula priorities

When writing formulas and developing sets of calculations (e.g., to calculate sales per year) I find it helpful to follow this order of priorities.

1. **Correct**: first and foremost, your formulas must produce correct results. Bear in mind, however, that in planning models we are calculating plan figures. These are only an estimate of what the numbers could be. As such, we should avoid trying to be too accurate. A good example here is tax calculations: tax regulations can be notoriously complicated and some of the rules often have no or only minimal impact for given planning scenarios. Therefore, write your formulas to give you *materially correct* results. That means any 'inaccuracy' in the result is not enough to change the user's opinion or decision.

2. **Understandable**: Your formulas must be understandable, for both you and the user. This is best practice to avoid errors in the development, testing and usage phases. This mirrors my rule: keep formulas short and simple. If necessary, spread your calculation into multiple steps, spread over multiple rows (or columns) to make it easier to understand.

3. **Short**: Understandable formulas are generally short, but do not make formulas short just for the sake of it, if they are then hard to understand.

Use the COUNT principle

COUNT stands for 'Calculate Once, Use Numerous Times'. That means if you need to use a value multiple times, you should calculate it just the once and then link back to that value in all subsequent calculations.

For example, in a model used to report daily sales to management, I had to compare the actual month-to-date sales with the planned month-to-date sales for each product. In each case, I calculated the planned month-to-date sales using the total planned sales for the month on a pro-rata basis e.g., given that (say) five sales days out of 20 (i.e., 25%) have passed. This percentage was obviously the same for all products, so it made sense to calculate it once and then link to the cell containing the result in all further calculations. This approach is more efficient than calculating the percentage again and again for each and every product and it speeds up calculations. This is particularly important for large or complex spreadsheets, which can take a while to calculate.

Another good example is **INDEX and MATCH**, which I explain in chapter 4 'Avoid common function errors'. Basically, if you need to retrieve various fields of data for a given data record, that data record is always in the same row, so you only need to calculate this row number once (with MATCH) for use in all INDEX formulas.

WHOLE SHEETS

Use consistent sheet structures

Sheets with consistent content (say, financial statements) should also have consistent structure. You can achieve this by simply copying sheets which you have already developed and tested, e.g., an integrated financial statements sheet for one group company can be copied for other group companies. In principle, you should develop and test once, then use multiple times. This approach offers similar advantages to consistent columns and rows, but on a larger scale: it is more efficient to develop and easier to understand and use than if each sheet is different.

2.3. RULE #3 – USE A CLEAR, CLEAN, CONSISTENT DESIGN

You should ensure your whole workbook design has the 3C attributes: clear, clean and consistent for a professional look and feel which is pleasant and easy to use. Put another way, make sure you only work with good-looking models ☺. This will not only make your spreadsheets easier to develop and use, but it will also help you avoid errors.

THE 'BROKEN WINDOWS' THEORY OF SPREADSHEET DESIGN

Some of the following tips relate to a consistent look and feel, both throughout an individual spreadsheet but also across spreadsheets used within an organisation. That includes things such as a consistent use of colours and column widths. Does this help users and avoid errors? I think it does... a professional-looking spreadsheet is easier to use, and it encourages users to take more care of the data and the calculations in it. In a messy spreadsheet, who cares? This is simply the criminological 'broken windows' theory applied to spreadsheets. To paraphrase the Wikipedia definition, 'the theory thus suggests that modelling methods that target minor crimes such as messy formats, garish colours and hard-coding help to create an atmosphere of order and reliability, thereby preventing more serious errors.'

So now let's cover the best practice advice to avoid 'broken windows' in your spreadsheets.

USE A CONSISTENT FONT

Use a consistent font and no more than, say, two or three font sizes for the whole model. I use Calibri – a modern, sans serif font – typically in size 10 for most of the spreadsheet and 12 for titles.

 **how2excel tip**

Set a default font

You can set the default font and size for all new spreadsheets under File, Options, General.

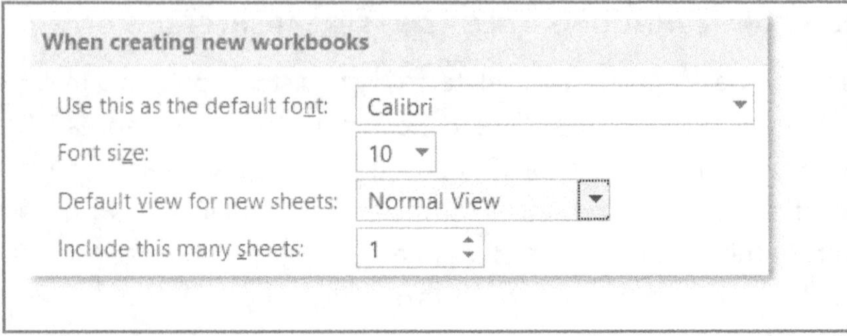

DEFINE AND USE A COLOUR SCHEME

Use a consistent colour scheme and cell formatting for the whole model, ideally one you have developed before and can readily use in all your models. You can customise colours in Excel, so these are always available for fonts, cell backgrounds, graphs etc. Start by going to the 'Page Layout' ribbon, 'Themes' section, 'Colors' and selecting 'Customize colors' at the end. Select a colour and change it as you see fit. Once you are finished, you can give it a name in the 'Name' box and save it.

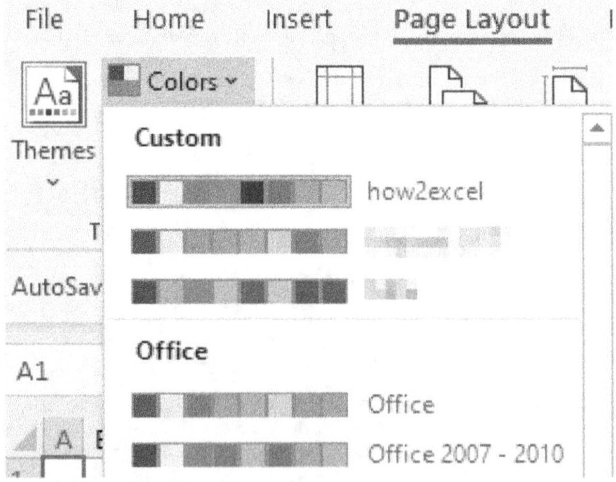

You can then 'install' the predefined custom colours in any Excel file you wish simply by going to the 'Page Layout' ribbon, 'Themes' section, 'Colors' and clicking on the relevant colour scheme name (in the screenshot above: 'how2excel'). For existing files with existing colour schemes, this may not work out the way you want, so you have may have to simply accept the existing colour scheme.

DEFINE AND USE CELL STYLES

Clear and consistent use of cell formatting makes it easier for both spreadsheet developers and users to interact with your file and can also be used to prevent undesired changes to formulas and model structure.

- **Define:** You can define styles with specific formatting on the 'Home' ribbon under Styles. Click the down arrow and select 'New cell style then define desired fill colours and borders.

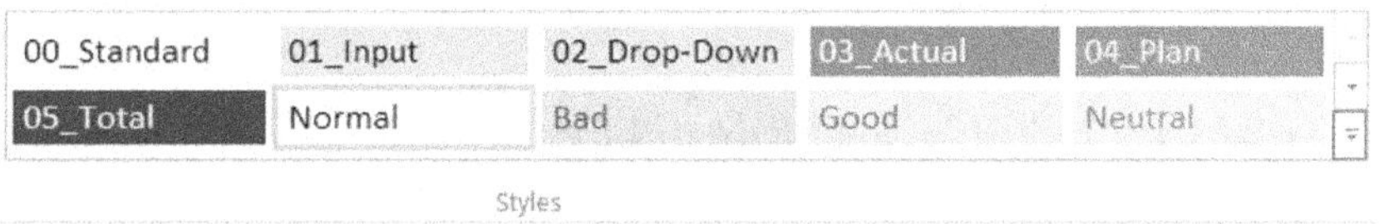

For inputs and drop-down cell formats, please turn off the cell protection property i.e., uncheck the 'locked' option shown below.

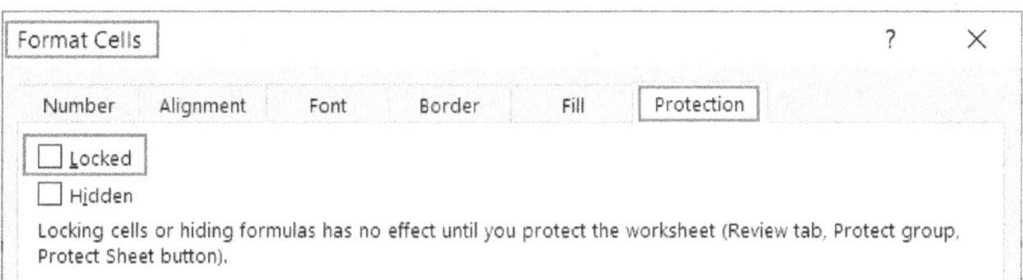

Please note the comment shown in the dialog box above: 'Locking cells ... has no effect until you protect the worksheet.' We will cover this point in more detail under Golden Ground Rule #4.

- **Save template**: To make the custom styles available in other spreadsheets, first save them in a separate file called e.g., 'My Template'. Make a copy of this file and rename it for each new Excel analysis or model. Alternatively, you can copy the styles into a new file either by copying a sheet from the template file into the new file (the styles are copied as well) or by clicking the down arrow in the styles box in the new file and selecting 'merge styles' from the template file, which must be open.

- **Use styles:** Use the styles for appropriate cells e.g., input cells by selecting the cell(s) and then selecting the relevant style on the ribbon.

If you do not want to create your own styles, you can use mine (just download the file which accompanies this book) or one from a professional organisation. For example, modelling company F1F9 has defined its own standard called FAST which includes cells styles and also keyboard formatting shortcuts and other rules to help create consistent, reliable spreadsheets, which you may find useful.

USE THE FOUR KEY DESIGN PRINCIPLES

The four key design principles are: contrast, repetition, alignment and proximity. Some of these we have already met, but here is a quick summary, as applied to spreadsheets.

- **Contrast:** You can use contrast to good effect to help users readily identify sections, for example by always having section headers (such as 'Sales', 'Costs', 'Assets') in bold. This is like having chapter titles in a book and it serves a similar purpose: it makes sections clearer and therefore the content is easier to navigate and 'read'.

- **Repetition:** We can also call this consistency. 'Consistency is key' is one of my favourite spreadsheet-based rules. It is efficient for both spreadsheet development (develop and test a section once, use many times) and for users (understand one section, understand all those which are consistent). It also helps avoid errors e.g., for cross-sheet links. When formulas are copied to the right, consistent columns help reduce the risk of errors e.g., of incorrectly linked periods.

- **Alignment:** Generally speaking, make content easier to read by keeping text left-aligned and numbers right-aligned. These are the standard settings in Excel and also help you identify if numbers are formatted as text, which can result in errors. Positive and negative numbers can be better aligned so that the units always appear directly underneath each other, which makes it easier to scan them and perform mental arithmetic (please see sub-chapter 5.1 'Build in error checks and a master check' for details on how to do this).

- **Proximity:** Content that belongs together should be near each other. So, do not have a big gap of blank rows in the middle of (say) your sales calculations. By contrast, content which does not belong together should be further apart. So, gaps between sections (e.g., between P&L and balance sheet) should be larger than any gaps within a section (e.g., between different assets). Here you can use two blank rows instead of one. This represents 'white space', which makes the start and end of sections clearer and so makes your spreadsheet easier to understand and use.

Note: The four design principles are Contrast, Repetition, Alignment and Proximity, that have an easy-to-remember acronym. For more details, see The Non-Designer's Design Book by Robin Williams (she defined these principles) or the excellent Clarity and Impact by Jon Moon (only available from his website www.jmoon.co.uk/book.cfm) where the principles are explained along with plenty of other useful tips.

CLEARLY MARK INPUT CELLS

Use a unique style for input cells – I use a light grey background and a thin white border. You will see this in many of the example screenshots I use in this book. This makes it obvious for users which cells are for inputs, which makes the model easier to use and reduces the risk of (user) error. In other models I have seen, pale yellow is a common background colour for input cells, often combined with blue text. But do not use text colour alone to mark input cells – if they are empty, you cannot see the text colour and it is therefore not obvious that it is an input cell. Whatever colour you decide to use, make it clear for users (e.g., in a colour key on the cover sheet) and be consistent in using it.

Other cells should not be changed by end-users. This can be enforced using cell locking and sheet protection which I cover under Golden Ground Rule #4 below.

 **how2excel tip**

Find and format inputs cells which you forgot

What if you forgot to format your input cells as inputs? Do not worry, help is at hand.

- Select the block of cells which may contain inputs

- Press F5 (Go To), special, constants, ensure the 'numbers' box is ticked; possibly deselect ticks for text etc., click 'OK'

- Excel then marks all the cells which contain numbers.

You can then click on the 'inputs' style to mark them all at once. It may be necessary to additionally add the style to other input cells that are empty or any containing formulas to calculate the input value as Excel cannot detect these as inputs. If your spreadsheet is well constructed, however, these should be relatively easy to identify as they should be in the same rows as input cells with inputs. If, like me, you like to use the keyboard, you can also use the shortcut F4 or Ctrl Y (repeat last action) to mark the additional (blank) cells as inputs after you have selected them.

USE GRIDLINES WHERE HELPFUL, BUT MINIMISE USE OF CELL BORDERS

Gridlines are the faint grey lines around each cell which Excel gives you as standard. If you do not want them, you can simply turn them off on the relevant sheet(s). Go to View, (Show section), and remove the tick in next to the Gridlines option. This method has the advantage that it is easy to turn the gridlines on and off as you or your user sees fit. I generally leave them on for tables of data so you can more easily trace rows across the page with your eye but turn them off for key output sheets as it makes them 'cleaner', but I appreciate it is somewhat a matter of taste.

Some spreadsheet developers colour their cells white, so the borders disappear. I do not recommend this as it is not easy to get them back if you want to. If you have multiple colour formatting on your worksheet, which is often the case, you cannot simply select all cells and make the fill colour 'no fill' since then all colours are removed.

Cell borders are similar to but different from gridlines. They can be added by users to mark the outlines of selected cells and effectively overlay the gridlines with another colour or style. I often see all data cells with black borders. As a general rule, I do not recommend using borders for whole blocks of cells as this makes it very difficult to see which cell is selected, something which is vital to be able to do efficiently when you are reviewing your spreadsheet and checking precedents and dependents, a topic we will cover in more detail in chapter 6 'Find and correct errors'. It also goes against the design recommendation from visualisation guru Edward Tufte (Tufte, 2007) which is to minimise non-data ink. Borders are not data and therefore should not be used since they do not add any information. You already have the gridlines, and these should suffice in most cases. If you wish, you can instead optically split different blocks of data from each other by simply using blanks rows or columns. This has the advantage of adding white space, a design element which makes the page look more appealing.

2.4. RULE #4 – RESTRICT ACCESS, INPUTS AND CHANGES

Restricting access to spreadsheets helps prevent unauthorised reading and changing of files by untrained users. Restricting inputs and changes helps to reduce the risk of error. I therefore recommend all three approaches.

RESTRICT ACCESS

You should restrict access to spreadsheets by storing them in folders, for example on a server to which access is restricted to a specific department or management team and, if appropriate, protecting them with a password. Mircosoft has hidden this function; to find it, please open a file, select 'Save as' then click on 'Tools' next to the 'Save' button.

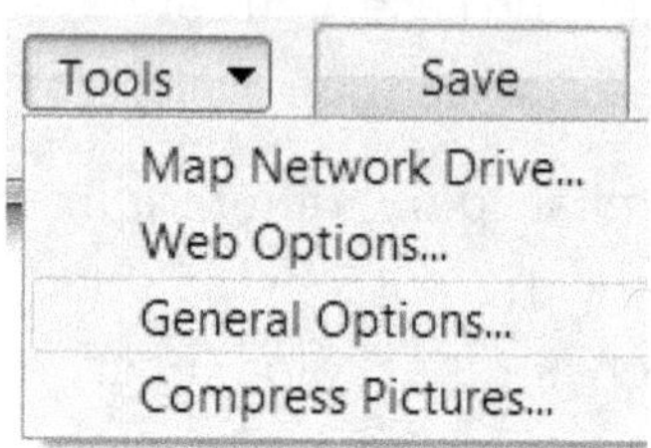

Next, select 'General Options' and enter either a password needed to open or modify the file, as appropriate. You then have to confirm the password and finally, you may have to confirm that the existing file (without password protection) should be overwritten. Excel files with password protection are not 100% secure, but that is no reason not to use passwords since most people won't be able to access a password-protected file without the password.

So now imagine the scene: you have built a fantastic model following best practice principles but then you hand it over to the users... and they make a proverbial dog's breakfast out of it by inputting invalid data, changing valid formulas or overwriting them with numbers, inserting extra rows and columns for extra content, and marking lots of cells in high contrast colours. YUK! Not only does it no longer look good, but the risk that it contains errors has now also significantly increased.

So what can you do to stop such behaviours? There are two basic approaches:

Method 1: Restrict inputs using data validation

I'm a big fan of data validation and use this a lot to restrict data input to only valid entries. To do this, first select the relevant input cell(s) and mark these clearly with a predefined cell style so the user can immediately see that the cell is for an input or a drop-down list (restricted input); see Golden Ground Rule #3 for more details on cell styles. Then navigate through the menu: 'Data', 'Data Validation' to get the relevant dialog box.

Firstly, you must decide what to allow. As a default, this is 'Any value'. Select an option and complete the additional input fields, which then appear, to restrict the inputs which are allowed.

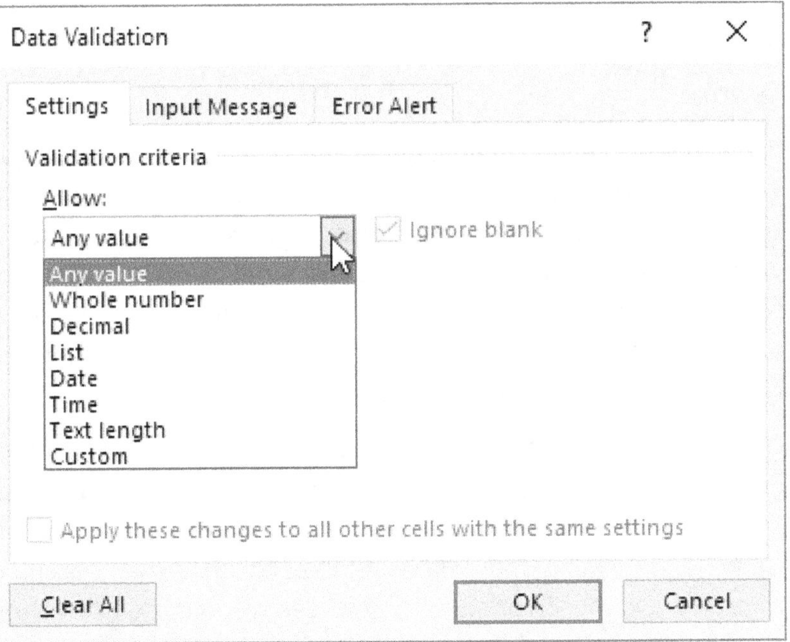

For example:

- Whole number: only integers from 1 to 5, e.g., for fixed asset useful lives.

- Decimal (values that may have digits after the decimal point): for example, only decimals with positive values (greater than or equal to zero) for sales prices or only negative values for planned cash outflows for rent or tax payments.

- List: probably my favourite! Allows you to allow only entries from a list. Either enter the list in the dialog box itself e.g., yes,no (with separators – either commas or semi-colons depending on your language settings – but no spaces between list items) or link to a list in the model e.g., scenario names. I use this one regularly – it saves you typing (or mistyping!) entries into the dialog box, and it is also easier to update the source list in the spreadsheet, for example if you change the name of a scenario from (say) 'best case' to 'optimistic case'.

- Text length: good for product codes or postcodes which have a fixed length.

- Custom: another of my favourites! A Boolean formula is required. This must start with an equals sign (i.e., a formula) and be followed by a test which can be true or false (what you would typically type when using an IF formula). This is extremely flexible. For example, to ensure the data entered is a Monday enter this formula =WEEKDAY(C2;1)=2 where C2 is the cell with the data validation. You can use $ fixing here, if appropriate.

You can also complete the tabs 'Input message' and/or 'Error alert' to advise users what type of data they must input. This is useful because otherwise, if they input invalid data, they just get a standard error message saying 'invalid data' with no clue as to what is wrong and what is acceptable. On the 'Error alert' tab you can also decide what happens if input data does not meet the validation criteria. The default option is 'stop' i.e., the data is not accepted. Alternatively you can change this to a 'warning' or 'information'. For a warning, the user gets warned but can still go ahead – I use this for entries where I normally expect a negative value e.g., for a payment of taxes but which could, under certain circumstances be a positive value e.g., a tax refund. With the option 'information', invalid entries are always allowed; this makes little sense in my opinion.

If you selected the option 'list' under 'Allow', then clicking in a restricted input cell will now give you a drop-down arrow which enables you to select a predefined item from the list. In this case, I use a special cell style called 'drop-down' (a pale brown background with white borders) to clearly mark the cells optically.

Data validation and copying

When you copy cells with data validation, the data validation rules get copied too. You can also copy and special paste validation rules to existing cells. But beware: in this case the rules are not applied until someone enters a value (or a new value) in them. This can also be an issue if instead of manually typing data into cells the user copies and pastes the data in. Again, the data validation rules are not applied! The solution is to check this afterwards. Select the cells with the data validation you wish to check then use 'Data Validation', 'Circle Invalid Data'.

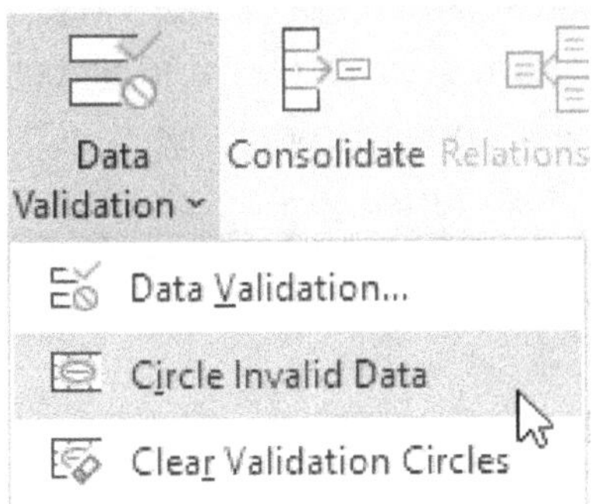

Invalid items are circled in red and can be corrected.

2. Follow Gary's Golden Ground Rules

Product	Sales
Alpha	278
Charlie	326
Foxtrot	353
Bravo	105
Total	1.062

The red circles disappear when you save the file or remove tracing arrows (see sub-chapter 6.1 'Standard Excel' – Formula auditing tools).

Method 2: Restrict or prevent changes using protection

Before you hand over your model to the users, you can protect sheets so that they can only change input cells and perform certain other restricted actions such as select cells and use filters. To enable this is a two-step process: (i) the cells must be protected and (ii) the protection must be turned on.

(i) Protect cells

All cells where changes will be prevented (i.e., changes will not be allowed) must be formatted as 'locked' and all cells where changes will be allowed (input cells and drop-downs) must be formatted as not 'locked'. To see the status of a given cell, select it, then format cells (shortcut Ctrl 1) and select the 'protection' tab, as shown in the screenshot below.

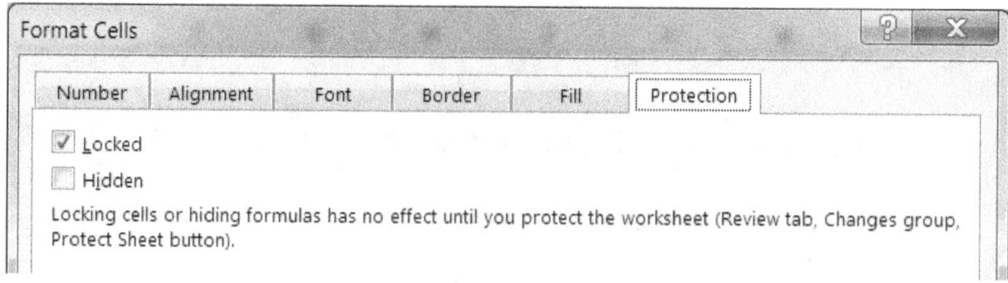

By default, all cells in a new workbook are locked. That means you need to unlock all input cells, including any drop-downs. It is best to do this as you develop your spreadsheet since unlocking input cells later is a time-consuming, error-prone process – you are bound to miss some and, consistent with Murphy's law, they will be exactly those cells the user wants to change.

The easiest approach to unlock input cells is to use cell styles, which I explained in Golden Ground Rule #3. I typically use one cell style for inputs and another for drop-downs with a different colour, both of which are unlocked, i.e., the 'locked' option box is not ticked. When you want an input or drop-down cell in your model, select the cell(s) and click on the relevant style name in the styles box on the home ribbon. The cells are then given the appropriate colour and are unlocked... simple and effective!

 **how2excel tip**

Turn on background error checking to identify missing protection

You can turn on background error checking for 'Unlocked cells containing formulas' under 'File', 'Options', 'Formulas', 'Error checking rules'. Excel then automatically marks any unprotected cells with a green corner, and you can then correct the cell formatting, as explained above.

The protection tab offers an additional option, 'hidden'. This allows you to hide the cell formula in the formula bar when the cell is selected. In the interests of transparency and understanding a spreadsheet, I do not recommend this option.

(ii) Turn protection on

This step is hinted at by Excel in the note underneath the protection settings. 'Locking cells ... has no effect until you protect the worksheet.' This is simple enough to do.

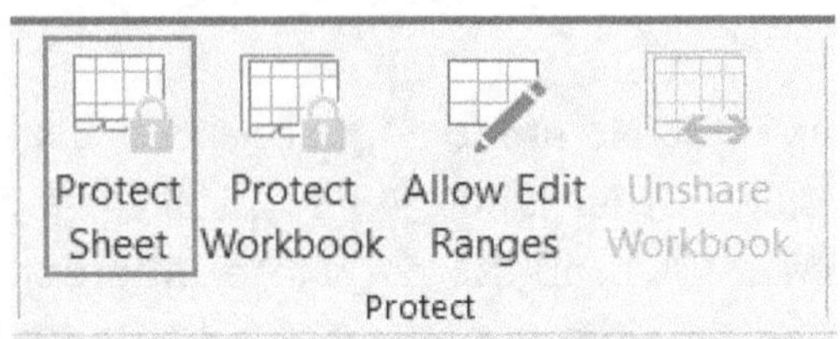

Select the relevant worksheet, navigate to the Review ribbon, click 'Protect Sheet', and possibly select what you want to allow. 'Select locked cells' and 'select unlocked cells' are allowed by default – generally sensible – but can be deselected. All other options are deselected by default but you can tick an option box in each case. One I generally allow is 'use autofilter', especially for data analysis files or in models with large input sheets.

The final step is to input a password, confirm the password (to avoid typos) and you are done. Obviously, you must remember the password, which can become a problem if you have lots of protected spreadsheets in use. You can therefore consider protecting the worksheet without a password to avoid problems.

Repeat for all further sheets in the model that you wish to protect. I am afraid there is no option to turn the protection on (or off) for all worksheets at once, so this task quickly becomes time-consuming and irritating. I therefore use a macro to protect all worksheets in a workbook and another to unprotect them all. Please see my how2excel example files available at https://www.knott-consulting.com/en/book/.

The VBA macro code is in the main file 'how2excel – example calculations and macros'. The 'protect sheets' macro also solves another problem with protected sheets: by default, you cannot open and close row and column groupings on protected sheets (an Excel bug), which can be very frustrating. As well as protecting sheets, the macro provided specifically enables the opening and closing of row and column groupings.

Either way (manual or macro), I strongly recommend using the same password for all protected worksheets in a single spreadsheet otherwise the pain of password management or the risk of forgetting a password becomes too great.

Protect the workbook structure

On the Review tab next to 'Protect Sheet' there is an icon for 'Protect Workbook'. This enables you to prevent users changing the structure of a spreadsheet i.e., moving, deleting or adding worksheets, which may be worth considering.

2.5. RULE #5 – WRITE INSTRUCTIONS FOR USERS

Especially for files which need to be updated regularly, I have found it extremely helpful to have a sheet in the file with step-by-step instructions for users, which could include yourself! You don't have to remember all the steps in your head, and it prevents you forgetting anything. This is especially helpful if the file is not updated frequently (e.g., only once a year) or if the regular spreadsheet user is absent or leaves and the work has to be completed by someone else.

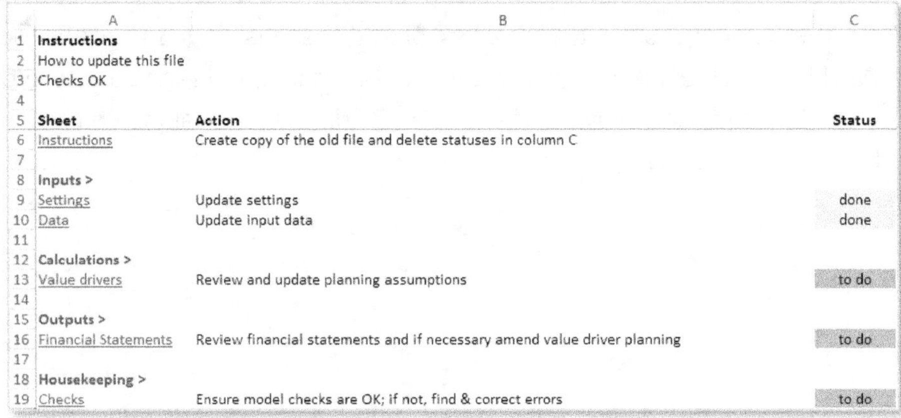

I include at least three columns as follows:

1. **Sheet:** For each action necessary, first create a hyperlink to the relevant sheet:
   → 'Insert', 'Hyperlink', 'Place in this document', select sheet and if appropriate, amend the default cell reference A1 – where the cells 'jumps to' when you click on the hyperlink.

2. **Action:** Briefly describe the necessary action.

3. **Status:** Add a cell with the status such as 'to do', 'done' or 'n/a'. You can make the status cells more user-friendly as follows. I recommend that you format one status cell first, then copy it to all the other action steps.

- **Use data validation:** Only allow predefined statuses to be selected. Select relevant cells then navigate to → 'Data', 'Data Validation', 'Allow': List, under 'Source' enter 'done,n/a,to do' (no spaces and without the speech marks), then click OK. Selecting a status cell now gives you a drop-down arrow which enables you to select a predefined status from the list. See Golden Ground Rule #4 above for more details on this useful functionality.

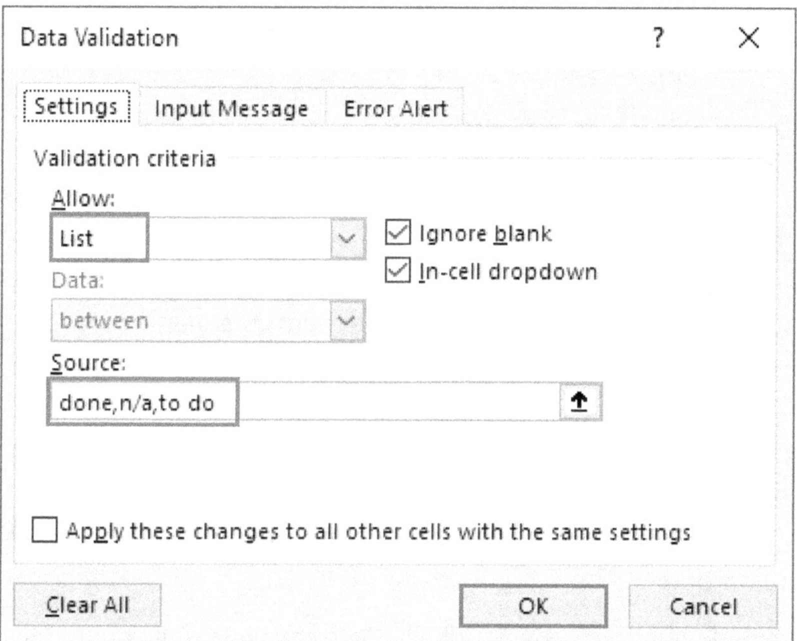

- **Use conditional formatting:** Format the status cells with a light red background colour (as the default colour) and then use conditional formatting to automatically colour the status cell light green if the status is changed to 'done' or 'n/a' → 'Home', 'Conditional Formatting', 'New Rule', 'Format only cells that contain', 'Cell value', 'equal to', enter 'done' (without speech marks); 'Format'..., 'Fill', green; repeat these steps for Cell value, equal to, 'n/a'.

This technique can be used anywhere in your model where you want to highlight specific data, e.g., Checks not OK (bold & red) or values over a certain threshold, say EUR 500k.

Additional columns can be used for relevant check results, references to source files or helpful screenshots or comments.

I have found the use of instruction sheets invaluable in practice. They reduce errors as you do not forget any steps. And the status clearly shows you and anyone else who opens the file what still has to be done to complete the update.

2.6. BEST PRACTICE CHECKLIST

Rule #1 – Use a clear, logical workbook structure

Decide what worksheets you need, give them clear names and get them in order.

- Spread content logically over clearly named worksheets

- Separate inputs, calculations and outputs

- Organise worksheets into sections to reflect data flow from inputs to outputs

- Include a cover sheet, ideally with hypertext links to facilitate navigation

Rule #2 – Keep your worksheets as clear and simple as possible

Ensure each worksheet is clearly laid out and easy to use.

- Use a logical structure within each worksheet

- Use consistent columns, row, formulas and whole sheets

- Formulas

    - Ensure calculations flow from left to right and from top to bottom

    - Use the KISS principle: keep it short and simple

    - Follow formula priorities: (i) correct, (ii) understandable and (iii) short

    - Follow the COUNT principle: Calculate Once, Use Numerous Times

---

Rule #3 – Use a clear, clean, consistent design

Ensure the whole workbook has a clear, professional look and feel.

- Use consistent (company-defined) fonts, colours and styles

- Use the four key design principles: contrast, repetition, alignment and proximity

- Clearly mark all inputs, for example as grey cells

- Minimise non-data ink e.g., borders

Rule #4 – Restrict access, inputs and changes

Ensure that only authorised users can access and change your spreadsheet and that inputs are valid.

- Restrict access to the spreadsheet using folders with restricted access and passwords

- Use data validation where relevant to help ensure inputs are valid

- Consider protecting workbooks so that changes can only be made in input cells

Rule #5 – Write instructions for users

Ensure that users know what to do and in what order e.g., how to update the model with new data.

- Create a worksheet with an action list for users to follow

- Add a status column to ensure progress is clear

3. Learn from horror stories

'It's good to learn from your mistakes.
It's better to learn from other people's.'
Warren Buffet, American investor and philanthropist

Now you know the Golden Ground Rules which, if you use them, should not only make your spreadsheets easier to develop and use but should also help prevent errors. But good error prevention is more than that... in this chapter, you will learn about errors which have actually occurred. This will develop your error awareness and you will also learn how to avoid such errors in your own spreadsheets with further best practice methods and techniques.

We will look at over 20 examples of real spreadsheet errors that have occurred, some of them repeatedly, and see how they arose, as far as can be ascertained from information in the public domain. These were mostly reported in the press or on the Internet, and many are collected on the website of the European Spreadsheet Risk Interest Group (EuSpRIG) at: http://www.eusprig.org. Some examples are from my own personal experience.

For the public cases, I include details as they have been reported. I sadly cannot validate or investigate the errors described because the underlying spreadsheets are usually not available. But I use the cases as examples to show the kind of errors that can occur and explain how these can be avoided.

I have grouped the stories into different types of error, such as mistakes in usage or copy and paste errors. In each case, I first describe the background, the error and the outcome. I then quote one or more internet sources in case you wish to read further details. Some cases have been widely reported, others less so. Lastly, but most importantly, we then look at how you can avoid such errors. In general, you need to use best practice techniques when developing your spreadsheets and be aware of potential pitfalls when using certain Excel functions. I assume you are sufficiently familiar with the basic Excel functions I mention. In some cases, however, I go into more detail to ensure you understand the problem and my proposed method to avoid such errors.

In many cases, I use screenshots of example calculations, which are purely illustrative. You can access the examples depicted in the free bonus files available at https://www.knott-consulting.com/en/book/.

There are two key reasons why I do not use the original model to illustrate the error: (i) the original model is almost never available and (ii) the error would in most cases not be easy to depict in a compact and easy-to-understand format in a book. Therefore, I have created example spreadsheets which show the kind of error that may have occurred. I say 'may have' because the descriptions in the public domain are often sketchy and lack real detail (the company which created and/or suffered from the error presumably does not want to look completely idiotic by revealing the error in all its glory) and the public reporting often focuses on the dramatic rather than the technical aspects of each case. I nevertheless hope that these illustrative examples will help you understand the kinds of Excel error that can and do occur, that can and do have real and material consequences, and (most importantly) I hope that my techniques will help you avoid such errors in your own work.

Awareness and training are essential ingredients for effective error prevention, so please read on for more of both...

3.1. MISTAKES IN USAGE

Data and calculations may be correct, but incorrect Excel usage can still lead to errors that are expensive and embarrassing, and can even cause health issues, as the following examples show. The good news is that these kinds of error are mostly easy to avoid; you just need to be aware of the risks and act accordingly.

PUBLIC HEALTH ENGLAND (PHE) LOSES NEARLY 16.000 COVID-19 CASES

Background: During the COVID-19 pandemic in 2020, PHE was responsible for collating results on confirmed COVID-19 cases from various laboratories and publishing statistics. The data was also used as part of the test and trace programme to inform people who had been in contact with infected persons that they needed to self-isolate (stay at home), with the aim of restricting the spread of the deadly disease, which was without a cure or a vaccine.

Error: Data from at least one lab was passed to PHE in the form of a comma separated variable (CSV) file, which can be opened and read in Excel. CSV files have no limit on their length, but Excel files do. It appears that PHE was using an old file version of Excel (XLS) which had just over 65.000 rows. Later Excel file formats (e.g., XLSX) can handle over 1 million rows. Whatever the format, it is an upper limit, and it was only a question of time before new tests at the bottom of the CSV lab files were effectively no longer read and saved by Excel.

Outcome: Nearly 16.000 confirmed COVID-19 cases were lost in processing and reporting. They therefore went missing from the statistics, which were used to help decide on official policy and practices to help restrict the spread of the disease. Perhaps more worryingly, the 16.000 people who had been confirmed to have the disease and people they had been in contact with – approx. 50.000 in total, including high-risk groups – were not informed and told to self-isolate and restrict contact to others. This increased the risk of further infection and the number of infected persons.

Sources: https://www.theguardian.com/politics/2020/oct/05/how-excel-may-have-caused-loss-of-16000-covid-tests-in-england

https://www.bbc.com/news/technology-54423988

How to prevent such errors:

1. **Decide if a spreadsheet is the right tool for the job:** This is the very first prevention step, which we covered in sub-chapter 1.1 'Decide if a spreadsheet is the best solution'. Some critics have argued that Excel was not suitable for the PHE task and another program, e.g., a database, would have been a better choice. This may well be true and PHE may even have been aware of this. But time was pressing, and they needed to get a system up and running that was more efficient than the previous paper and pen solution(!). Ultimately, it was not PHE's decision to use Excel that was the real problem, but a failure to realise the limitations of the version they were using and to either upgrade or adapt their use of it accordingly.

2. **Get trained or use suitably trained staff:** This is the second prevention step, which we covered in sub-chapter 1.2 'Get trained'. All staff using spreadsheets benefit from formal training. For high-risk tasks, spreadsheet development should be assigned to more experienced persons.

3. **Test your tool:** We cover this topic in detail in sub-chapter 5.3 'Get an independent review and test', but we can say here that all spreadsheets should be tested before use and that the amount and detail of testing should reflect the complexity and importance of the individual file. This task: important, therefore: more testing.

4. **Consider using Power Query:** According to Microsoft, there is no limit to the size of data tables that can be handled by Power Query. Not only that, but Power Query can also be used to automate the data import e.g., from CSV files stored in a specific folder and process these in flexible and innovative ways using the DAX language. Please bear in mind however, that even in modern Excel versions such as Office 365, the maximum number of rows filled to a worksheet is still 1,048,576. So, if you have data sets which are (or potentially could be) larger, you will need to use Power Pivot to produce your outputs. This does not really represent a restriction in

most cases, since by summarising the data in just the way you need it, Power Pivot tables can provide an overview of your outputs which is better for reporting (as in this story) or decision making.

BARCLAYS HAS TO BUY UNWANTED CONTRACTS

Background: During the financial crisis of 2008, Barclays agreed to buy certain contracts from the failed Lehmann Brothers, but not all of them. There were nearly 200 contracts that Barclays did not want to buy. All Lehmann Brothers' contracts were listed in a spreadsheet. The 200 contracts which Barclays did not want to buy were included but were hidden and there was an explanatory footnote.

Error: A PDF was created from the spreadsheet and included as part of the purchase contract. Unfortunately, the 200 contracts that Barclays did not want were included and the footnote was excluded from the PDF.

Outcome: Barclays had to buy nearly 200 contracts that they did not want.

Source: https://incisive.com/spreadsheet-error-horror-stories/

How to prevent such errors:

1. **Do not use hidden rows or hidden columns:** They are bad practice! They often get overlooked but are typically still included in calculations such as SUM. If they are unhidden, any special status ('not wanted' in this case) is then lost.

2. **If appropriate, group data into separate blocks:** In this case, simply including 'Contracts purchased' (e.g., rows 5 to 500) and 'Contracts not purchased' (e.g., rows 505 to 700), with a clear title for each group, would have avoided this issue.

3. **Alternatively, include extra column(s) for filtering:** In this case, that could have been 'Contract purchased?' with 'yes' or 'no' entered

for each row. This column can then be used for filtering (e.g., before printing), SUMIFS and pivot tables.

4. **Use row or column groupings where necessary:** If you 'must' hide rows (or columns), then use Excel groupings: here it is more obvious that rows or columns exist but are not visible due to the + symbol at the left-hand side indicating the grouped rows (or at the top for grouped columns). But please combine this with one of the two tips above.

The next two examples also involve hidden columns, but in these cases the problem was not faulty presentation but disclosure of confidential information.

UNICREDIT DISCLOSES CONFIDENTIAL RESULTS IN ERROR

Background: UniCredit, Italy's biggest bank, created a spreadsheet with historical data, which was uploaded to its website and also sent to analysts and investors.

Error: The spreadsheet also contained preliminary and incomplete figures for its third-quarter results in two columns which were hidden, but accessible.

Outcome: Users of the spreadsheet could unhide the columns and see results data before they were supposed to. In addition, the hidden data was incomplete and not ready for release.

Source: https://www.businessinsider.de/unicredit-accidentally-emails-q3-results-a-fortnight-early-2017-10?r=UK&IR=T

Similar error: BOEING SENDS CONFIDENTIAL EMPLOYEE DATA

Background: A Boeing employee had problems formatting a large spreadsheet.

Error: The employee sent the spreadsheet by e-mail to his wife to ask for her help. It contained personal information on around 36,000

employees including dates of birth and social security numbers in hidden columns.

Outcome: Boeing had to report the 'loss of control' data protection breach to the state attorney and suffered a loss of reputation when the story was widely reported. The company wrote to every employee to advise them of the details, offer help and advise them to be on the lookout for any fraudulent use of the data due to identity theft. The story was particularly embarrassing as Boeing also sold a software package called Cipher, which could have prevented the error, but a spokesman explained that the company only required the software to be used for classified work.

Sources:
https://www.bizjournals.com/seattle/news/2017/02/28/boeing-discloses-36-000-employee-data-breach.html

https://www.theregister.co.uk/2017/02/22/boeing_employee_emails_personal_info_36000_colleagues/

How to prevent such errors:

1. **Do not be complacent:** Please do not think, 'that would ever happen to me or my company!'

2. **Get trained or use suitably trained staff:** In the Boeing case, the user sent the file because he needed help. Trained users are less likely to need assistance. If they do, trained users should be more aware of the risks and seek help within the company, so there is no need to send the file to anyone outside.

3. **Use a separate file with restricted access:** Keep confidential, draft or sensitive data in a completely separate file to other data. Protect the file with a complex password (see sub-chapter 2.4 'Rule #4 – Restrict access, inputs and changes' for more details on password protection) and store it in a folder to which only authorised people have access.

4. **Do not hide data**: As noted previously, do not use hidden rows or hidden columns: These are bad practice and the hidden data, which may be sensitive or confidential, can easily get overlooked and distributed to unauthorised people in error, as the above examples show.

If you must send the data to someone else, please use the following methods.

1. **Separate confidential data from the rest:** Ensure that (i) the confidential data and (ii) the data to be sent (let us call them outputs) are on different worksheets. If necessary, restructure your spreadsheet to achieve this. This is a condition for the following techniques and helps reduce the risk of error.

2. **Send only PDFs:** If the recipient only needs to read the data and not work with it in Excel, save the output sheets (none containing restricted data, of course) as a PDF. To do this, first set the print ranges and settings on the appropriate sheets. Then select all the relevant worksheet name tabs and use the menu 'File', 'Save as' and select file type *.pdf. Browse to a suitable folder then save the PDF file. Open and check the PDF before sending.

3. **Create a 'sent version':** If the recipient has to work with the data in Excel and not just read it, then you must remove confidential, draft or sensitive data which they are not entitled to see before sending the file. Here is a method I have successfully used many times. The main file you work on is the 'master' file. Before you send any part of it, create a 'sent version' excluding the restricted data as follows.

    a) Identify the necessary worksheets that you need to send. Typically, these are just the output sheets from the master file, which may rely on, but do not contain, the restricted data.

    b) Copy the worksheets to be sent to a new workbook. The easiest way to do this is to select all the relevant worksheet name tabs, then right-click on one tab and select the 'move or copy' command. Under the heading 'To book:' select 'new book' and, very importantly, check the 'create a copy' option box at the bottom. If you forget to do this, the sheets are not copied but are moved, and are no longer part of the master file. If this happens, move them back into the master file using the same technique and try again.

c) Save the new file with the copied worksheets as '… sent version.' In this new file, break the links to the master version to avoid potential connection errors arising and also to avoid the use of formula editing tools (see chapter 6 'Find and correct errors') to potentially identify data in the source spreadsheet. To do this, go to: 'Data', 'Edit Links', select the master file name, 'Break Link'. Then save the file again.

Note: 'Break links' works best on simple, direct links to cells in another spreadsheet. If the formulas are more complex, it does not always work. There are also other types of links that cannot be broken by this method: range names, graph data, data validation rules, conditional formatting and pivot tables. Please see my blog at https://www.how2excel.com/en/get-rid-of-those-annoying-links/ for more details and advice.

d) You can write a macro to automate the above steps if it is something you need to do regularly but be sure to test this thoroughly and always open and check the 'sent file' before sending.

e) Now record those steps as a list of instructions on a sheet in the file (see sub-chapter 2.5 'Rule #5 – Write instructions for users') detailing the steps necessary to prepare a 'sent version' of the file for distribution. Then advise all users to follow these instructions each time they need to create a new 'sent version'.

If your worksheets contain pivot tables that use the restricted data then it is vital that you also follow the advice given after the next two horror stories, since it is remarkably easy to access the underlying data. Unfortunately, many people are unaware of this as you will see.

BLACKPOOL TEACHING HOSPITALS REVEALS EMPLOYEE DATA

Background: Blackpool Teaching Hospitals wanted to provide details of its equal opportunities and decided to post an entire spreadsheet with details online.

Error: The spreadsheet, which was online for 10 months, contained pivot tables, which with a simple double-click would reveal underlying details of every employee including sensitive personal data.

If your file contains one or more pivot tables then please be aware that as a default, the underlying data is stored with the pivot table. This can simply be accessed by double-clicking any element in the pivot table to see the related underlying data. So even if you do not include the source data sheet in the posted or sent version of your spreadsheet, the data is still there. This is particularly important to know if the data is confidential, such as here: employee data.

After being made aware of the problem, Blackpool Teaching Hospitals commented: 'nobody knew that Excel could do things like that.' This was despite the fact that the Commissioner had already penalised two other trusts for similar disclosures and had highlighted the risks in his blogs. Perhaps the teaching hospitals should extend their teaching to include Excel 😊.

Outcome: Blackpool Teaching Hospitals were fined £185,000 by the Data Protection Commissioner.

Source: http://www.eusprig.org/horror-stories.htm identifier POB1603

Here is a similar error:

KENSINGTON AND CHELSEA COUNCIL (KCC) DISCLOSES PERSONAL DATA

Background: In June 2017, there was a large fire at Grenfell Tower, a block of flats in London, in which 71 people died. The case generated a lot of media interest including the possible use of empty properties in the borough to house survivors. Several reporters asked KCC, in whose borough the flats were located, for details of all empty properties in the borough under the Freedom of Information Act which KCC supplied in a spreadsheet.

Error: According to the BBC, the spreadsheet included a pivot table which contained 'the names and addresses of 943 people who owned vacant homes in the borough … and three high-profile names were published by a national newspaper.'

A report into the incident found that the KCC employees who provided the spreadsheet had not received adequate Excel training.

Outcome: KCC was fined £120,000.

Source: https://www.bbc.com/news/uk-england-london-43785626

How to prevent such errors:

1. **Be aware of the risks:** An awareness of the issue is half the battle. You are now aware, so what can you do to win the other half?

2. **Use PDFs:** Save the pivot table results to a PDF and send that instead of the spreadsheet. Simple and effective! See the previous horror story for more details on how to do this.

3. **Create 'sent versions':** If the data has to be provided as a spreadsheet file, then to avoid the risk that users can access underlying, sensitive data, replace the whole pivot table in the sent version with values, as follows:

   a) Make a copy of the file to post or send so that you can keep the original file in case you need to review or update it.

   b) In the copied version, copy the whole pivot table. Then paste, paste values (or paste special, values) to replace the pivot table with values only. Now the underlying data is no longer accessible because it is no longer a pivot table, and the file size is also smaller. Unfortunately, this also means that users cannot modify the pivot in the sent version e.g., using filters or slicers but at least your sensitive data is safe.

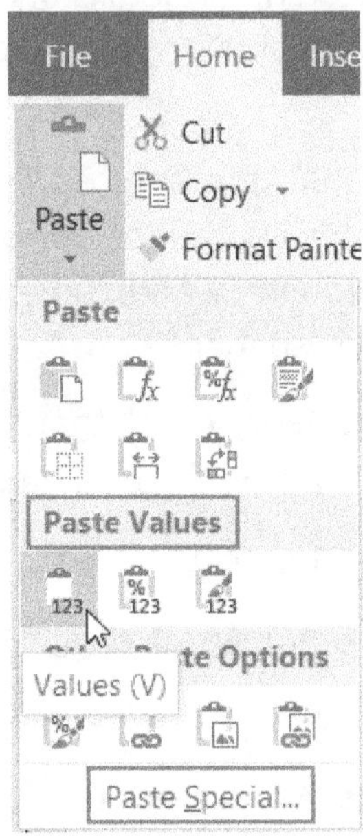

4. **Do not rely on pivot table options:** A hopeful-looking potential solution using pivot table options is sadly ineffective. You can right-click in the pivot table, select PivotTable options and on the 'Data' tab, deselect both 'Save source data with file' and 'Enable show details'. Sadly, this does not solve the problem because the user can change these settings back again unless you protect the sheet. If you do that, the user of the sent version cannot change the settings but also cannot modify the pivot table e.g., using filters of slicers. So, the effect is the same as the copy-value paste solution but riskier, for example in case a user guesses or breaks the sheet protection password.

US COUNTY MISSES $1 BILLION PROPERTY IN TAX ASSESSMENT

Background: Kern County in California, USA needed to assess properties for tax. The listings of properties and values used for this purpose were maintained in a spreadsheet that needed to be maintained as changes occurred.

Error: One year, the person responsible used the wrong version of the spreadsheet and so missed a valuable oil field belonging to Occidental Petroleum worth $1.26 billion. With an effective tax rate of around 1% p.a., this property should have generated around $12 million tax each year.

Outcome: If the error had not been noticed, the county would have had $12 million less to spend on things such as firefighters, law enforcement and other public services. In this case, however, there was a happy end (from the county's point of view). The error was found and corrected in a timely manner.

Source: http://www.eusprig.org/horror-stories.htm identifier FH1201

How to prevent such errors:

Before we get into prevention of errors caused by a lack of proper version control, let us quickly look at how important this seemingly mundane topic is. Felienne Hermans, assistant professor at Delft University of Technology, has studied spreadsheets and found that, on average, a spreadsheet has a life of around five years and about twelve people will use it (Shueh, 2014). In that lifetime, the spreadsheets will change and so it is important to have a robust system to keep track of the versions, so that all users know which is the latest version, where it is stored and who may work on it at any given time. So, version control is important, but is it a problem in real life?

The Kern County story shows that version control can be a real problem with real consequences. In addition, a detailed analysis of spreadsheets in use at Enron indicates they too had issues regarding version control. In the aftermath of the Enron scandal, Hermans carried out an analysis of nearly 16,000 spreadsheets in use there and related e-mails (Hermans, 2015). As noted previously, Enron may not be representative of companies in general, but the analysis certainly makes interesting reading. In her review, Hermans found that spreadsheets were often passed around in e-mails. Over 20% of the e-mails concerning spreadsheets were asking about new versions, updates or changes. This suggests that spreadsheet versions were not well controlled and hence there was a risk of using an incorrect version.

Now let us move on to the prevention advice.

1. **Store spreadsheets on the server or in OneDrive and do not send via e-mail if you can avoid it:** If you always save the latest version of a spreadsheet on the server or in a (shared) OneDrive folder and are using the other tips noted here, then authorised users can directly access the latest version and can recognise it as such. In addition, OneDrive has great automatic change history.

    By contrast, if spreadsheets are sent by e-mail, it requires time and effort to distribute them. You may forget to include a user who needs the file, or you may send it to someone unauthorised by accident. On top of that, a user can never be 100% sure he has the latest version without asking. The Enron mails suggest this can cost a lot of time and energy. Human nature being what it is, the user may simply use the version they have, which may be outdated, and this can lead to error. If you do have to send spreadsheets via e-mail (e.g., because developer and user do not have access to a common server), then the other controls noted here become even more important.

2. **Use an agreed folder structure:** I find the following works well:

    a) Model: Use a folder for the spreadsheet called (e.g.) 'Model' or 'Spreadsheet analysis' for clarity. There should be only one version of the workbook here – the current version.

    b) Previous versions: Always move older, completed versions to a sub-folder called e.g., 'Previous versions' or possibly 'Sent versions' if you have to send spreadsheets via e-mail.

c) Old drafts and working versions: Always move older draft copies (back-up copies created during development and testing) to a sub-folder called 'old'. These should not be used by anyone, and the folder name should make this clear. They are only for use in case you need to recover data or formulas from an older draft version.

3. **Use an agreed model naming convention:** This should include:

a) Model date: Although you can see a date and time for each file in Windows Explorer, this is the date the file was last saved and not necessarily the last time it was updated. I prefer to write the date in 'reverse order' i.e., year-month-day so I can sort archive versions in Windows Explorer.

b) Model name: For example, Project Apple, ABC financial model or XYZ cash forecast.

c) Model version number: I find this helpful for file management as every file version has its own name which can be spoken or written about, e.g., 'Please find attached version 2.3 of the Group Planning Model with the following changes: X, Y and Z. This replaces previous versions. Please update the planning assumptions and send back to me.' (e.g., as version 2.4.) Add 0.1 to the version number for each new version or jump to the next whole number if you make larger changes e.g., you just added a new entity to the group planning model. I also enter the version number on the cover sheet (see sub-chapter 2.1 'Rule #1 – Use a clear, logical workbook structure').

d) If appropriate, include any major changes in the file name e.g., 'with expansion capex'.

Here is an example file name which follows these tips: 20xx-10-28 Project Spring v2.3 with new cost estimates

4. **If files are sent back and forth, be clear who has the 'master version':** If responsibility for a file changes back and forth between

different persons such as the spreadsheet developer and the business user, then you must be very clear who has the 'master version' at any time. Only this person may amend the file. Here I find it helps to include a version number in the file name for clarity (see above). So just by looking at file names, you can see which one is the later version. Do not rely on the file save dates shown in Windows Explorer, as these can be misleading if someone opens and then resaves an older version – it then gets a current (save) date and time.

3.2. INCORRECT INPUTS

Simple errors such as an incorrect input can cause mayhem and cost real money, sometimes large amounts. And even if the data looks right, incorrect formatting may cause values to be ignored.

TOO MANY OLYMPIC SEATS SOLD

Background: The London Organising Committee of the Olympic and Paralympic Games (LOCOG) used a spreadsheet to manage and sell seats for events at the 2012 Olympics.

Error: The number of available seats for the synchronised swimming event was entered in the spreadsheet as 20,000. Unfortunately, there were only 10,000 seats available. A simple typo with a 100% error rate.

Outcome: LOCOG had to apologise profusely to affected sports fans and tried to get them to accept tickets for alternative events. Where this failed, they had to upgrade them to major events at a significant loss.

Sources: https://blogs.oracle.com/modernfinance/12-of-the-biggest-spreadsheet-fails-in-history

https://www.quickbase.com/blog/spreadsheet-horror-stories

How to prevent such errors:

1. **Obtain and store source documents:** We can generally split data into actual data, plan data and planning assumptions.

   a) **Actual data** such as, in this example, the number of seats available, or the number and capacity of wind power turbines in a wind park or the sales values from the last three years are facts and should be available in source documentation. In these examples, that could be a seating or wind park plan (detailed pictures) or prior year financial statements.

   b) **Plan data** such as planned costs may well be available in formal offer documents from potential suppliers or in signed contracts with actual suppliers.

   c) **Planning assumptions** may be documented in e-mails or meeting minutes or could be based upon prior year or prior project (actual) data.

   Store all source documents with the spreadsheet file in a suitable sub-folder.

2. **Clearly mark input data and quote sources:** Mark input cells consistently – I use a light grey background (see sub-chapter 2.3 'Rule #3 – Use a clear, clean, consistent design) and ideally collect all input data on an 'inputs' or 'assumptions' worksheet. For each significant data input or model assumption, document the source e.g., in a 'Source' column. This should ideally be a source document, which you have saved (see above), or alternatively the date and person who gave you the value and maybe a comment e.g., 28. Oct. 20xx CFO John Brown based upon recent discussion with engineer.

3. **Clearly mark any missing, uncertain or unknown inputs:** An additional technique here is to clearly mark any inputs that are uncertain or unknown, including test data entered during development and testing where final data is not yet available. For example, you can make the text red or the background yellow.

Ideally, make a list of such data, review this at least once and update the data before model completion. Then get it checked, ideally by an independent expert, before final use.

4. **Increase the visibility of significant values by showing them on the dashboard or cockpit:** That way, more people get to see them and can challenge them if they appear to be incorrect. If the significant value represents a planning assumption such as the dividend pay-out ratio or scenario selection (best, base or worst case), the value on the dashboard could become the input that feeds into the rest of the model. In this case, it may be appropriate to rename the sheet from 'Dashboard' (just outputs) to 'Cockpit' (inputs and outputs). This represents great functionality for users: they can check and amend key assumptions or switch scenarios and see the effect on key results all without leaving the cockpit sheet. (See sub-chapter 2.1 'Rule #1 – Use a clear, logical workbook structure' for more details.)

5. **Double-check key inputs:** Get your key inputs double-checked by an independent person against the source files and correct or follow up, as necessary.

6. **Add checks on totals:** If you get individual data items in a calculation sheet by linking to a source sheet or possibly an external file, the totals in source and destination sheets should agree. Add a check to make sure this is so. We cover this kind of check in more detail in sub-chapter 5.1 'Build in error checks and a master check'.

FIDELITY FORCED TO CANCEL A DIVIDEND

Background: Fidelity manages investment funds for investors. For the Magellan Fund, they used a spreadsheet to calculate the expected dividend for 1994 as $4.32 per share.

Error: The spreadsheet user forgot a minus sign when entering a capital loss of $1.3 billion, which was then treated as a gain of $1.3 billion, i.e., an error of $2.6 billion.

Outcome: As a result, the expected profit per share was greatly overstated and Fidelity was forced to cancel the dividend distribution for the fund when they spotted the error while making checks before the final pay-out.

Sources: http://catless.ncl.ac.uk/Risks/16.72.html

https://www.cio.com/article/2438188/eight-of-the-worst-spreadsheet-blunders.html

How to prevent such errors:

1. **Implement checks and controls early in your process:** Do not wait until just before final pay-out before double-checking your calculations but build them in from step 1. This is what Fidelity decided to do after this error occurred. They said, 'We have taken several steps designed to ensure that this error should not happen again. We will subject initial estimates to the same rigorous verification process that we use in preparing the distributions that the funds actually pay. This will include a thorough review not only by our own fund accountants but also by the fund's treasurer and independent auditors. In addition, estimates will be reviewed by each fund's portfolio manager.' Sounds good, if actually put into practice.

2. **Use separate rows for positive and negative number inputs and data validation:** In this case, you could have one line for capital gain and another for capital loss. The row labels should help users think about whether the input is a gain or a loss. Then use data validation (see sub-chapter 2.4, 'Rule #4 – Restrict access, inputs and changes') to ensure the inputs for gains are positive and those for losses are negative and give an informative error message if this is not the case.

   We now discuss further supporting checks that can help prevent input, calculation or usage errors associated with plus/minus signs.

3. **Define and use a sign convention consistently:** I recommend that you always represent sales, profits or cash inflows as positive numbers and costs, losses or cash outflows as negative numbers. This means you can always simply add up numbers in a profit and loss account (AKA income statement) to calculate the P&L or net cash flow. This avoids adding a loss when you should have subtracted it (as in this horror story): the sign makes it clear and you can always add it; you do not have to wonder whether to add or subtract it, which is both unclear and error-prone.

    In several cases I have seen a line in the P&L simply called 'Interest', which represents the net result of interest costs less interest income, which is usually a (net) cost. The value is shown as a positive number and, since it is a cost, it is then deducted in calculating the profit. In some cases, however, the net interest figure is interest income. In this case, the value must be shown as a negative value because it is deducted to calculate profit. To (have to) show a profit as a negative value is totally confusing and can only lead to misunderstanding. Someone could see 'interest' with a negative sign and change the formulas to add it when calculating profit. Result: confusion and error. Don't do it! Always calculate income as positive numbers and costs as negative numbers. Then either (i) show interest income and interest costs on separate lines in the P&L or (ii) show the net result in one line called e.g., 'Net interest income(+)/costs (-)'. The sign will indicate whether the net result is income (positive) or costs (negative). A similar approach for capital gains in the depicted story could have helped prevent the error or may have allowed it to be detected earlier.

4. **Construct your spreadsheet to reduce the risk of sign errors:** To determine figures in your spreadsheet you generally need input data and calculations. In general, I find that users find it easier to enter inputs as positive numbers. You should then take this into account when calculating figures e.g., for the financial statements. For example, you can calculate the COGS based upon the units sold

and the average cost per unit, both as positive value inputs. The formula to calculate the COGS is then = -(units sold x average cost per unit). Note the minus sign at the start of the formula, which creates a cost figure with a negative sign according to the logic explained above. There is no need for the user to remember to enter a minus sign when entering the inputs. If you require negative inputs, use data validation to ensure you get them.

5. **Review results:** Always sense-check your results (for more details see chapter 5 'Detect errors'). That is what Fidelity decided to do in light of the error that had occurred. If any odd-looking figures are, in fact, correct, add comments to help users understand.

KODAK FORCED TO RESTATE RESULTS

Background: Kodak used a spreadsheet to calculate pension and employment termination benefits.

Error: The data for one employee had too many zeros so his calculated severance payment was an incredible $11 million too high.

Outcome: As a result of the error, Kodak had to restate two quarters of financial results.

Sources: https://blog.caspio.com/5-of-the-most-terrifying-excel-spreadsheet-horror-stories-weve-ever-heard/

https://www.cio.com/article/2438188/enterprise-software/eight-of-the-worst-spreadsheet-blunders.html

How to prevent such errors:

1. **Use data validation:** We have covered this great control before, basically restrict the entries in key fields to allowable values, e.g., in this case values up to (say) $100,000. While this should help, it is not fool proof as you can copy and paste values from elsewhere into cells with data validation and then the validation rules are not

applied. Therefore, it's wise to have additional checks and controls in place, such as the following.

2. **Sense-check your data:** If you have a table of data, scan the values to spot and investigate any odd amounts that are not consistent with other values.

3. **Implement controls outside the spreadsheet:** If a spreadsheet calculates amounts to be paid (as in this case), additional controls should be implemented e.g., a formal review and sign-off by a suitably senior person prior to payment.

    This case also raises the subject of how best to present values. Here are some tips which you can follow to both improve clarity and reduce the risk of errors.

4. **Agree on and clearly state the currency and units in use:** The Kodak case sounds to me like it could be a classic case of mixing values in dollars and values in thousands (or millions) of dollars. Another potentially easy mistake to make is to add values in different currencies. Such errors are not so obvious when the exchange rate between the currencies is near to 1. You must convert all values to your spreadsheet 'reporting currency' first before you can use them in calculations. For both of these potential errors, the approach is the same. As noted in sub-chapter 1.3 'Plan your spreadsheet', it is essential that you decide on your reporting currency and units at the model planning and design stage (before model development) and also clearly state the units in use, especially where inputs are not standard e.g., another currency. The key here is to (i) avoid inconsistencies which could cause errors, (ii) make any inconsistences very obvious by clearly stating the units and (iii) restrict the length of numbers to make them easier to enter, use and interpret, which leads me to my next point.

5. **Do not use too many digits:** Please do not show values more accurately than thousands of dollars/pounds/euros and especially not with two decimal places (i.e., cents or pence). In planning

models, nobody can plan that accurately; using such units gives a false sense of accuracy. And such numbers make it harder to 'read' and assess results and find errors.

	20xx	20xx
	EUR	TEUR
Sales	4,852,689	4,853
COGS	(2,911,613)	(2,912)
Margin	**1,941,076**	**1,941**
Overheads	(1,455,807)	(1,456)
Profit before tax	**485,269**	**485**
Tax	(145,581)	(146)
Profit after tax	**339,688**	**340**

Look at the example shown above, which shows the same profit and loss statement first of all in whole Euros and then again in thousands of Euros (TEUR). Which column is easier to understand? The second column wins hands down. This is because the average number of digits shown per number (significant figures) in the Euros column is 6 or 7 and in the TEUR column it is just 3 or 4, which is much easier to read and comparing years also becomes much easier.

6. **Make exceptions if these are justifiable:** For some accounting calculations, especially payments or reconciliations, it may be appropriate or even necessary to calculate to the nearest cent or penny. A payment amount to the nearest thousand or million will not be accurate enough in many cases.

    You can also make an exception for some calculations of financial statement positions (so-called value drivers) e.g., planned sales = sales price times quantity sold in each period, or planned personal costs = average cost (including employer contributions) per full-time equivalent (FTE) for each period (e.g., a year) times the number of FTEs. Here it is often 'more natural' to use whole dollars/pounds/euros for average prices or personnel costs. In the example below, sales prices per unit are entered in whole euros and are around 100 euros in each period. The values are easier to enter, read and interpret.

	A	B	C	D	E	F	G
1	SALES (TEUR)	Units	Year 1	Year 2	Year 3	Year 4	Year 5
2	Sales price per unit	EUR	100	104	108	112	117
3	Quantity sold	Units	10,000	10,200	10,404	10,612	10,824
4	Sales	TEUR	1,000	1,061	1,125	1,194	1,266

If the sales price were, however, to be entered in TEUR, the necessary input values of e.g., 0.100 and 0.104 TEUR would be cumbersome to handle and to interpret. This raises the risk of error, and this may have played a role in the Kodak case with salary as an input in severance payment calculations.

If you do make an exception for certain inputs, then please ensure you clearly label the relevant section with the correct units, e.g., EUR for the sales prices in the above example. For consistency and to reduce the risk of error, I recommend you calculate results (e.g., sales per period in the above example) in the standard units for the spreadsheet – either thousands or millions of dollars/pounds/euros – so that these results can be linked further in the workbook without needing to be converted to different units elsewhere.

In summary, choose suitable units for your data, be consistent and be clear, especially for any deviations from the model standard. And always use the model standard units for results.

TUNNEL MODEL UNDERSTATED COSTS BY OVER 1M EUR

Background: The city of Gießen in Germany used a spreadsheet to plan the costs of a tunnel under a train track to be used by pedestrians and cyclists.

Error: The model included various costs totalling 2.5 million euros. These cost values were supplied by the German train operator. The city assumed they were gross values, including VAT, when in fact they were net values, excluding VAT.

Outcome: As a result of the error, the actual costs were around 500 thousand euros higher than planned. To add insult to injury, cost overruns added a further 600 thousand euros to the total capital expenditure. Administrators admitted that the case was 'not a gem' for the city.

Source: https://www.welt.de/wirtschaft/article176803436/Stadt-Giessen-verwechselt-brutto-mit-netto.html

How to prevent such errors:

1. **Do not assume:** This case reaffirms an important point I made earlier: do not assume. Instead, check and validate your data.

2. **Know your business:** In this case, not only was the assumption incorrect, but it was also inconsistent with normal B2B (business to business) practice where costs quoted by suppliers are usually net figures, since the VAT on top can be reclaimed by the purchasing company and does not therefore represent an additional cost. But, as they say in Germany 'trust is good, control is better'. So especially with large amounts, it is better to ask a 'stupid' question ('is that figure gross or net?'), than to assume and get it wrong.

3. **Document and check the sources of inputs and assumptions:** As recommended previously, use an extra column in your spreadsheet to document data sources and get someone else – ideally an expert – to check at least the key values e.g., the main cost figures (in this case). This gives you a second chance to catch any errors. The reviewer should also challenge key planning assumptions, such as the number of sales made by each sale force employee p.a. You can compare these to historical actual data for the company or division in question and/or relevant industry data (if you can get them). This is especially useful for the percentage of sales spent on R&D or on marketing in particular industries, for example. We cover this idea

in more detail in sub-chapter 5.2 'Review and test your spreadsheet' when we look at reviewing and testing.

SCHOOL LOSES 30,000 POUNDS FROM BUDGET DUE TO FORMAT ERROR

Background: A UK school governor submitted a budget, which he had calculated in Excel using data extracted from the accounting system.

Error: A 30,000 pounds number in the budget spreadsheet was formatted as text and so was not included in the total funding request. This is because some Excel functions such as SUM simply ignore text entries and do not report an error. The school governor said he knew that numbers could be formatted as text but there do not appear to have been any checks to identify the error.

Outcome: The school lost out on the relevant sum of money.

Source: http://www.eusprig.org/stories.htm story 067

How to prevent such errors:

In the following explanations I will refer to numbers formatted as text as 'text numbers'. These not only cause problems with mathematical operations such as SUM or AVERAGE. They can also cause errors when using lookups (e.g., VLOOKUP or MATCH) or SUMIFS if you are searching for a number, but the source data contains text numbers, or vice versa.

These kinds of error can also arise with dates, which are really just numbers (the number of days since 1st January 1900) formatted to look like a date. The regional settings can cause a date to be treated as text e.g., if your source data has full stops between date elements such as 07.10.2020 but these are not recognised as date separators by Excel due to your regional settings, which specifies a slash symbol and expects 7/10/2020.

1. **Use Excel background checks:** Excel offers a number of automatic checks, which you can turn on or off under 'File', 'Options', 'Formulas',

'Error checking' (turn them all on or off) and 'Error checking rules' (turn individual rules on or off). For error checking rules which are turned on, any cells which fail a check are then automatically flagged by Excel with a green corner.

In the example below, cell B4 has a green corner.

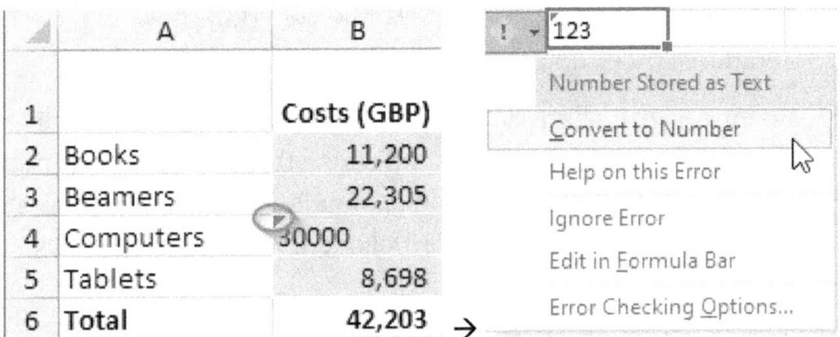

When you select the cell, an exclamation mark appears. You can find more information by hovering over the exclamation mark. Here Excel tells you 'The number in this cell is formatted as text or preceded by an apostrophe.' Clicking the exclamation mark gives you a drop-down with a list of options including a suggestion to correct the error, here 'Convert to Number.'

If you have multiple cells with the same error, you can apply the correction to all of them at once by first selecting all the cells, then applying the correction suggested by the exclamation mark.

2. **Correct the cell formats:** Formatting the cells as numbers is, sadly, not enough as Excel only applies the format when you enter data and not retrospectively. If you have only a few cells to correct, you can (additionally) press F2 (edit mode) then enter, to get Excel to apply the number format.

   The better option is to mark the whole column and use Data, Text to Columns, a very useful approach which we cover in more detail below.

3. Learn from horror stories

I cover Excel background check options in more detail in sub-chapter 6.1 'Standard Excel'. As I explain there, however, I find this option gives too many false positives i.e., it gives a warning when there is no error e.g., product codes with leading zeros must be formatted as text even though they are 'numbers'. This leads to the 'cry wolf syndrome', and you can start to ignore such warnings, including any which really are errors. Therefore, I have a few additional tricks up my sleeve...

3. **Do not 'right align' cells with numbers:** As a default, Excel left aligns text and right aligns numbers, so there is no need to manually align them. The default settings should make 'text numbers' more obvious as they will appear left aligned, not right aligned, like this:

	A	B
1		Costs (GBP)
2	Books	11200
3	Beamers	22305
4	Computers	30000
5	Tablets	8698
6	Total	42203

If you format the numbers with thousand separators (which I recommend, to make numbers easier to read), such an error should be even more obvious as 'text numbers' are both left-aligned and have no separators, like this:

	A	B
1		Costs (GBP)
2	Books	11,200
3	Beamers	22,305
4	Computers	30000
5	Tablets	8,698
6	Total	42,203

The 'text number' sticks out like a sore thumb and can be corrected. Even if a whole column contains text numbers, this should still be easy to identify, if you understand and follow this tip.

4. **Check your totals:** We cover check formulas in detail in sub-chapter 5.1 'Build in error checks and a master check' but here is a good place to have one if your input data (e.g., from a system report) also includes a total. In the screenshot below, we have copied in individual values and the total. We can check this total with a check formula to see if the total shown equals the sum of the individual amounts. In this case, the check formula identifies an issue.

◢	A	B	C
8		Costs (GBP)	[Cell] Formula
9	Books	11200	[B9] 11200
10	Beamers	22305	[B10] 22305
11	Computers	30000	[B11] 30000
12	Tablets	8698	[B12] 8698
13	**Total**	**72203**	[B13] 72203
14	Check	30,000	[B14] =B13-SUM(B9:B12)

The above tips help you identify that you have a problem. How do you then fix it? You have to convert all the data to numbers. There are two ways to do this.

5. **Convert numeric data to numbers**

Method 1: Multiplication

You can generally convert your data to numbers by simply multiplying by 1 in a new column. This requires that you use an extra column but is ideal if you update your input data from time to time, because the corrections then happen automatically.

This trick generally works for numbers and often for dates. In the example below, we have a list of four payments with payment dates as inputs. The date of the third payment (cell B19) is formatted as text, which means a MATCH formula cannot find it (cell B25). In column C, we have multiplied the dates by 1 which converts them to numbers and the MATCH formulas then work correctly.

	A	B	C	D
16		Dates	Dates as numbers	[Cell] Formula
17	Payment 1	31/03/2020	31/03/2020	[C16] =B16*1
18	Payment 2	30/06/2020	30/06/2020	[C17] =B17*1
19	Payment 3	30/09/2020	30/09/2020	[C18] =B18*1
20	Payment 4	31/12/2020	31/12/2020	[C19] =B19*1
21				
22	Date	Pmt number	Pmt number	[Cell] Formula
23	31/03/2020	1	1	[C21] =MATCH($A21,C$16:C$19,0)
24	30/06/2020	2	2	[C22] =MATCH($A22,C$16:C$19,0)
25	30/09/2020	#N/A	3	[C23] =MATCH($A23,C$16:C$19,0)
26	31/12/2020	4	4	[C24] =MATCH($A24,C$16:C$19,0)

If a column can legitimately contain numbers and text e.g., customer account numbers which are sometimes just numbers but can contain one or more letters, you can amend the multiplication formula to read = IFERROR (cell reference *1, cell reference). This result can then be used for lookups or SUMIFS etc. As always, do not just assume such a trick will work; please test it.

	A	B	C	D
28	Customer	Account	Lookup a/c	[Cell] Formula
29	Able	123445	123445	[C29] =IFERROR(B29*1,B29)
30	Baker	156887A	156887A	[C30] =IFERROR(B30*1,B30)
31	Charlie	B789426	B789426	[C31] =IFERROR(B31*1,B31)

Method 2: Convert text to columns

This method does not require an extra column but is better suited for cases where the data will not be updated in the future as it must be applied for each set of data inputs. Just formatting the data, e.g., the whole column as a number does not work on its own. If you have only a few cells with text numbers, you can force Excel to recognise and apply the number format by selecting each cell in turn, pressing F2 and then enter. This becomes tiresome for lists longer than (say) five inputs.

In such cases, select the whole column (or the cells containing the data), in the menu select 'Data', then in the Data ribbon select 'Text to Columns' to start the 3-step wizard. In step 1 you must select the data type as either delimited or fixed width. Since we are not splitting the data, either option will do, so select next. Step 2 is irrelevant, select next. In step 3 you can select the data type. The default is 'General' which is great for numbers or 'Date', where you can specify the order of date month and year. The advanced option is great for defining the decimal and thousand separators used in the data as these can be different to your regional settings used by Excel. Finally select 'Finish' and your data is converted. When you get experienced with the tool, and if your data is just numbers without the complication of decimal and thousand separators, you may find you can start the wizard and then simply select finish without going through all the steps. Either way, please check your results.

3.3. HARD-CODED VALUES

This section is dedicated to a big 'no-no' of modelling: hard-coding. That means including a number that represents an assumption in a formula, e.g., a VAT rate or a cost increase of 5% p.a. Why is this bad practice? Because such numbers are not clear to users unless they click on a cell and look at the formula. And if the value changes, all relevant formulas need to be updated... which ones are they? Are you sure you can find and change them all? Even if you can, it is time-consuming and also time-wasting as there is a better way.

Sometimes a hard-coded number is intentionally used in a formula to alter the output to achieve a desired result. In real life, such behaviour could be called cheating. In modelling it is sometimes referred to as a plug. Whatever you call it, it is undesirable. We are not trying to develop electric cars here, so please avoid plug-in models!

DATA USED IN A POPULAR ECONOMICS BOOK IS NOT ENTIRELY RELIABLE

Background: *Capital in the Twenty-First Century* is a best-selling book from 2014 by leading French economist, Thomas Piketty. In it, he addresses questions about capital including the long-term evolvement of inequality. His book is based on detailed analyses of data from 20 countries reaching as far back as the eighteenth century.

Error: The *Financial Times* not only reviewed the book but also the underlying data which, to his credit, the author had made available. Unfortunately, they discovered that 'the data underpinning Professor Piketty's 577-page tome, which has dominated best-seller lists in recent weeks, contain a series of errors that distort some of his findings. The *Financial Times* found mistakes and unexplained entries in his spreadsheets... there are transcription errors from the original sources and incorrect formulas. It also appears that some of the data are cherry-picked or constructed without an original source.' (Giles, 2014)

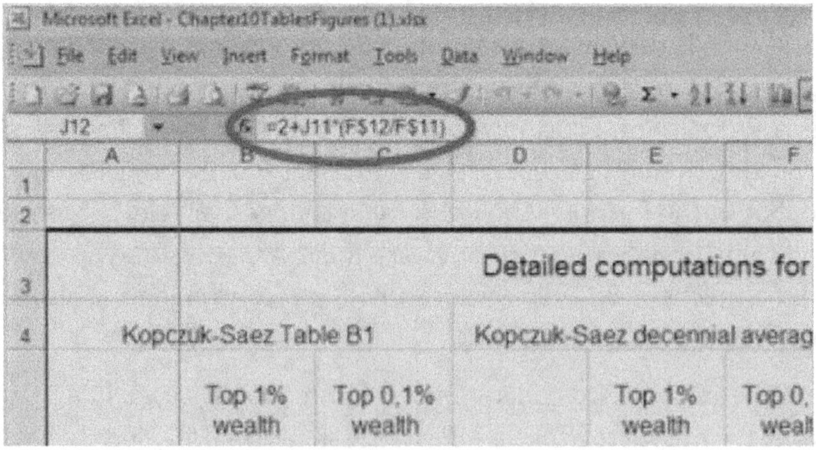

© *Financial Times*

In the screenshot above, taken from a video interview with the author of the *Financial Times* article, Chris Giles, we can see that in one formula, the number two has been added to the formula. The reason, Chris Giles explains, is 'because the result wasn't high enough and didn't fit what he wanted to show in his charts... There is quite a lot of this sort of thing in his spreadsheets'.

In a separate article, *Breaking Views* reports: 'For instance, Piketty's tables include a column calculating the share of wealth owned by the top 1 per cent in France. For the period from 1810 to 1960, he pulls figures from various raw data tables and multiplies them by a hard-coded factor. This is 1.05 in all cases except for 1910, where, without explanation, it is 1.08. For 1970, he simply writes in a percentage for the wealth share, rather than referencing one of the sets of source data. More recent years involve both approaches.' (Beales, 2014)

Outcome: The conclusions drawn by Professor Piketty in his book do not appear to be entirely supported by the data that he made available. In a response to the criticism, however, Professor Piketty claims that recent data more than support his conclusions.

Sources: https://www.ft.com/content/e1f343ca-e281-11e3-89fd-00144feabdc0

https://www.breakingviews.com/considered-view/piketty-spreadsheets-set-bad-excel-example/

How to prevent such errors:

1. **Do not hard-code:** Quite simple really!

2. **Always show data, assumptions, adjustments and factors clearly as inputs:** If you do need to make an adjustment for a legitimate reason, e.g., planned revenues will be increased by a one-off release of a provision, show this in a separate cell formatted as an input and reference this cell in the formula. In this way, any such adjustments are 'out in the open' and obvious to all users.

3. Learn from horror stories

Here is an example of common hard-coding I have seen when calculating amounts of tax – either corporate tax or VAT / sales tax.

	A	B	C	D	E	F	G
1		Year 1	Year 2	Year 3	Year 4	Year 5	[Cell] Formula
2	**Corporate Tax**						
3	Earnings before tax	100	110	120	130	140	[B3] ='P&L'!B7
4	Tax	(30)	(33)	(36)	(39)	(42)	[B4] =-B3*30%

In this example, we have the earnings before tax for 5 plan years in row 3 and the tax calculation in row 4. Here, the 30% tax rate is hard-coded in the formula. Such hard-coding is not visible when you just look at the results.

	A	B	C	D	E	F	G
1		Year 1	Year 2	Year 3	Year 4	Year 5	[Cell] Formula
2	**Corporate Tax**						
3	Earnings before tax	100	110	120	130	140	[B3] ='P&L'!B7
4	Tax rate	30%	30%	30%	30%	30%	[B4] 0.3
5	Tax	(30)	(33)	(36)	(39)	(42)	[B5] =-B3*B4

The screenshot above shows a corrected version. The tax rate is now clearly shown in an extra row of input cells in row 4 and these are referred to in the formulas in row 5. This approach has the advantages that (i) the tax rate inputs are clearly visible to users and can be easily changed if necessary, e.g., the government announces a change in the tax rate from next year and (ii) the formulas in row 5 do not have to be amended and remain consistent (part of Golden Ground Rule #3: Consistency is key), even if there is a change in the tax rate in any year. Both points help to avoid errors.

3. **Clearly mark temporary hard-coding used for test purposes and remove after testing:** Here is a technique I successfully use if I overtype a formula with a value in order to test my spreadsheet. I mark the hard-coded cell in bright yellow, so it is clear to me I have to change it back to the original formula once I have finished testing. Since my formulas are consistent, this is simply a matter of copying an adjacent cell and pasting it over the hard-coded value. If I have to check other sheets during the testing, I also mark the tab of the worksheet with the hard-coded value yellow.

3.4. SUM AND OTHER CALCULATION ERRORS

SUM... it is the simplest and probably the most used function in Excel. It is so simple, surely no-one can make an error here. Well, I am afraid users can if they incorrectly omit cells from a range when using SUM or a similar function such as AVERAGE as the following examples show. The good news is, such errors are easy to avoid if you use the methods explained below.

LARGE COSTS OMITTED IN CONTRACT PRICE CALCULATION

Background: Emerson Electric Co., a large technology and engineering company, used a spreadsheet to estimate the component costs of a contract bid for the U.S. Army Corps of Engineers for the construction of barracks at Fort Hood, Texas and to calculate the total costs.

Error: The sum of the total costs missed the cell for the electrical costs totalling $3.7 million. These costs were thus not considered. A review reported as follows: 'Our review of the record, including Emerson's computer-generated spreadsheets, confirms that the price at spreadsheet cell number D159 (for electrical work) was not included in the subtotal at cell number D160. Based on the format of the spreadsheet, it is clear that the $3,702,025 price at cell number D159 was intended to be included in the firm's subtotal price.' They therefore submitted a bid of USD 35.6 million, notably lower than other bidders and the government's own estimate.

Outcome: Emerson won the bid with their low price but was allowed to correct their price when, upon being asked to justify their low value, they discovered their error. They thus avoided an expensive loss. However, a competitive bidder, Roy Anderson Corporation, protested. Detailed proceedings followed, which presumably took up much time for the participants and the outcome was uncertain. All of this could easily have been avoided.

Sources:

https://www.gao.gov - article no longer available

http://www.eusprig.org/stories.htm story 025

How to prevent such errors:

1. Use AutoSum to help select the correct range

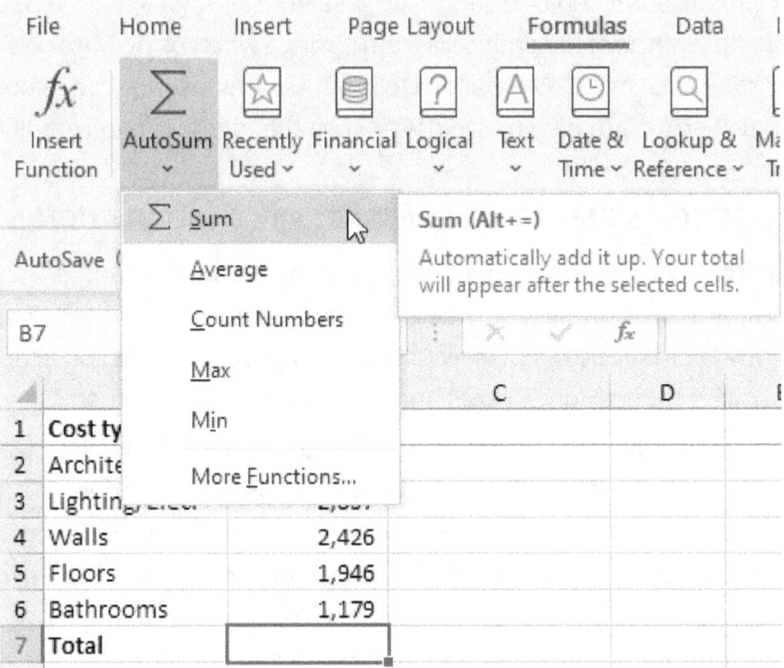

Select the cell where the SUM formula should be written, then click on the AutoSum icon in the formulas ribbon. For AVERAGE, COUNT, MAX, and MIN use the drop-down arrow first (see screenshot) and select the relevant function. Please single click the icon and check the range selected before accepting or amending it. If you simply double-click the AutoSum icon, the formula is entered without a chance for you to check the selected range.

If you simply want a SUM, you can also use the keyboard shortcut Alt = (or Alt Shift = if you need the shift button to type the equals sign). You can see this shortcut at the top of the tooltip in the screenshot above, but Excel shows this as (Alt + =) which I find misleading since you don't need the + symbol; (Alt and =) would be clearer or simply (Alt =), which I prefer.

You can also use AutoSum to SUM (or AVERAGE, MAX, MIN etc.) data in a row instead of a column.

How does AutoSum identify the relevant range? Excel first looks for a block of numbers in the column above the selected cell. There can even be blank lines between the end of the data and the selected cell. If it finds such a block, Excel assumes you want to SUM (or AVERAGE, MAX, MIN etc.) the column. If it does not find data there, Excel then looks to the left to see if there is a block of numbers in the same row. If so, Excel assumes you want to SUM (or AVERAGE, MAX, MIN etc.) the row.

Watch out! If your data has gaps or subtotals in it as the AutoSum can get these ranges wrong. So whichever way you use AutoSum (icon or shortcut), please check what range of cells Excel has selected and amend this if necessary.

The following tips apply to both sums (or averages etc) of rows and columns. For the sake of brevity, I will mention only rows and SUMs. Even if your SUM range is initially correct, errors can arise when you insert new rows of data. So here are my tips to avoid errors here.

2. **Avoid adding new data above the first data row or below the last data row:** New data added above the first existing data row will not be included in the SUM. Data added at the end may be added to the SUM range, but there is a risk that it may not. Therefore, avoid both. If you must add a new row here, remember to check the SUM formula ranges and amend if necessary.

3. **For added rows (or columns) of data, use automatic range extension:** From Excel 2013, Excel will automatically extend the SUM range if you insert a new row of data directly above the SUM. This avoids an error that cropped up a great deal in the past, so thanks a lot, Excel! For this to work, you have to have a least 3 items of data in your sum and the relevant option must be turned on, which it is by default. You can check the setting here: 'File', 'Options',

'Advanced', 'Extend data range formats and formulas'. Even with this handy feature, it is always best to set or check the SUM range yourself to be sure it is correct.

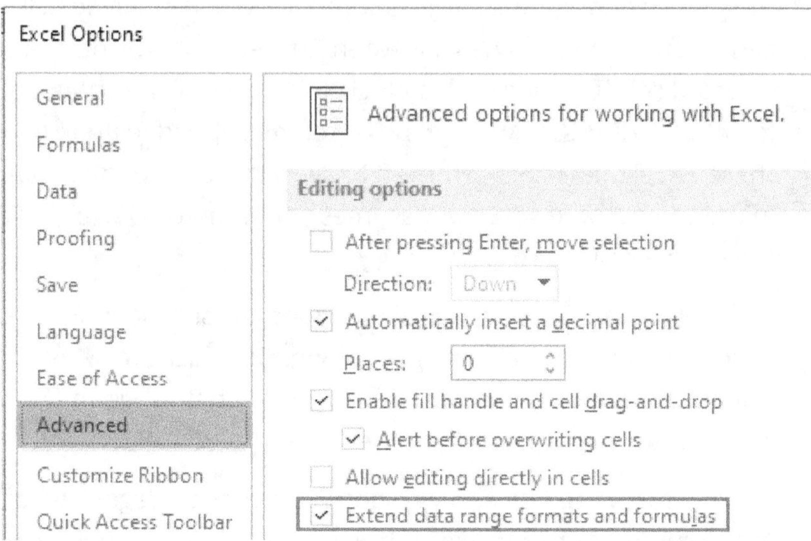

If you are using an older version of Excel or another spreadsheet program that does not do this, then use the following tip.

4. **Consider inserting a blank line before a SUM total:** Then include this blank line in the SUM range. This means that if you insert a new row of data after the last existing data row, the new data will automatically be included in the SUM total. To visually indicate that this blank line is not to be used for data entry, reduce the row height to, say, 8.

5. **Use an Excel table:** A alternative solution to all the above tips is an Excel table. There are some great advantages of converting your data into an Excel table, including reduced risk of sum errors.

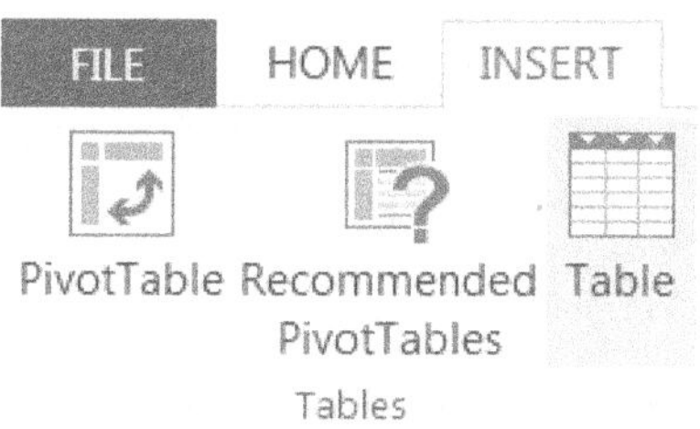

To convert your data: Select a cell in your data, then use the menu Insert, Table, or use the keyboard shortcut Ctrl T. Your data then gets a colour makeover and looks something like the screenshot below. If you want to change the colours, select a cell in the table and then use the new 'Table Tools', Design at the right-hand end of the Excel ribbon.

	A	B	C
1	Cost type	Costs (USD	[Cell] Formula
2	Architect	2,950	
3	Lighting/Elec.	2,837	
4	Walls	2,426	
5	Floors	1,946	
6	Bathrooms	1,179	
7		11,338	[B7] =SUM([Costs (USDk)])

If you create a SUM (or AVERAGE, MAX, MIN etc.) formula and mark all entries in the column, Excel creates a formula that refers to the column name, in the above example 'Costs (USDk)'. If you add a line at the end of the Table for new data, the sum formula automatically includes it. The sum formula can also be placed above or next to the table (which makes it easier to add extra data to the table). Another advantage of Excel tables is that formulas in your table are automatically copied to new rows.

6. **Keep formulas next to the data used:** If you need to know (for example) total costs, I recommend that you calculate the sum next to the data (above or below it) and then refer to this cell on any other sheet which needs to use it (calculations) or report it (outputs). This

approach makes formulas easier to understand and to review. If there is a (potential) error in the sum, you can check this more easily when the sum formula and the data are on the same sheet and not on different sheets. The next tip is strongly related to this one.

7. **Avoid cross-sheet calculations - use simple links only:** A formula referring to another sheet should be a simple link to a single cell and not contain any calculations, if at all possible. Logical, really, when you think about it. But I have seen many spreadsheets where this recommendation has not been followed, which made them difficult to review and understand. If you are using SUMIFS on one sheet to analyse data on another sheet, then you cannot apply this tip, but I recommend it in other cases.

Sometimes SUM errors arise in connection with double counting. We cover this type of error and also the function SUBTOTAL in sub-chapter 3.7 'Circular errors and mistakes in logic'.

WIDELY QUOTED ECONOMIC GROWTH STATEMENT BASED UPON INCORRECT CALCULATION

Background: Eminent academics Carmen Reinhart and Kenneth Rogoff produced a famous study in 2010 entitled 'Growth in a Time of Debt' and concluded that economic growth suffers when countries have public debt levels over 90% of GDP – growth levels are then just 0.1 % p.a. This result has been widely quoted as a reason why countries should reduce their levels of public debt.

Error: Other academics failed to reproduce the results, so Reinhart and Rogoff released their spreadsheet, which was found to contain an embarrassing error: average formulas did not cover all the data. This is one of the rare examples where we have details of the spreadsheet containing the error. The error can be clearly seen in the screenshot below which shows the range of cells referred to in a key formula. A number of countries including Belgium were omitted, which had a significant impact on the result.

◇	B	C	I	J	K	L	M
2			Real GDP growth				
3			Debt/GDP				
4	Country	Coverage	30 or less	30 to 60	60 to 90	90 or above	30 or less
26			3.7	3.0	3.5	1.7	5.5
27	Minimum		1.6	0.3	1.3	-1.8	0.8
28	Maximum		5.4	4.9	10.2	3.6	13.3
29							
30	US	1946-2009	n.a.	3.4	3.3	-2.0	n.a.
31	UK	1946-2009	n.a.	2.4	2.5	2.4	n.a.
32	Sweden	1946-2009	3.6	2.9	2.7	n.a.	6.3
33	Spain	1946-2009	1.5	3.4	4.2	n.a.	9.9
34	Portugal	1952-2009	4.8	2.5	0.3	n.a.	7.9
35	New Zealand	1948-2009	2.5	2.9	3.9	-7.9	2.6
36	Netherlands	1956-2009	4.1	2.7	1.1	n.a.	6.4
37	Norway	1947-2009	3.4	5.1	n.a.	n.a.	5.4
38	Japan	1946-2009	7.0	4.0	1.0	0.7	7.0
39	Italy	1951-2009	5.4	2.1	1.8	1.0	5.6
40	Ireland	1948-2009	4.4	4.5	4.0	2.4	2.9
41	Greece	1970-2009	4.0	0.3	2.7	2.9	13.3
42	Germany	1946-2009	3.9	0.9	n.a.	n.a.	3.2
43	France	1949-2009	4.9	2.7	3.0	n.a.	5.2
44	Finland	1946-2009	3.8	2.4	5.5	n.a.	7.0
45	Denmark	1950-2009	3.5	1.7	2.4	n.a.	5.6
46	Canada	1951-2009	1.9	3.6	4.1	n.a.	2.2
47	Belgium	1947-2009	n.a.	4.2	3.1	2.6	n.a.
48	Austria	1948-2009	5.2	3.3	-3.8	n.a.	5.7
49	Australia	1951-2009	3.2	4.9	4.0	n.a.	5.9
50							
51			4.1	2.8	2.8	=AVERAGE(L30:L44)	

Screenshot © *Washington Post*

Initial criticism of the conclusions from some economists was not directed at the formula error (at the time unknown) but at the causality. They argued that perhaps it was low growth causing high levels of public debt, not the other way around.

Outcome: When the formula error was corrected, the average growth rate for countries with public debt levels over 90% of GDP rose to 2.2% p.a., due to the inclusion of Belgium. This result no longer strongly supported the study's conclusion, but this has not stopped it being widely quoted and presumably used to guide national economic policies.

Sources:

https://www.washingtonpost.com/news/wonk/wp/2013/04/16/is-the-best-evidence-for-austerity-based-on-an-excel-spreadsheet-error/?noredirect=on&utm_term=.3112da3ab876

https://www.reuters.com/article/us-summers-lessons/column-the-lessons-of-reinhart-rogoff-idUSBRE9450CF20130506

How to prevent such errors:

Whether or not the causality argument holds, it is clearly better to ensure that your calculations are free of technical errors. The solutions to prevent such technical errors (items missing from a formula range) are basically the same as for SUM, repeated here for reference:

1. Use AutoAverage to help select the correct range
2. Avoid adding new data above the first data row or below the last data row
3. For added rows (or columns) of data, use automatic range extension
4. Consider inserting a blank line before an AVERAGE total
5. Use an Excel table
6. Keep formulas next to the data used
7. Avoid cross-sheet formulas and use simple links only

    On the subject of causality...

Always remember that correlation does not prove causality: When performing data analysis and comparing two sets of data, always keep in mind that even if changes are correlated, factor A may not cause factor B: it may be the other way around or the correlation may be due to a third factor such as time or weather. For example, wearing a t-shirt does not cause you to buy more ice-cream. Both are caused by warm weather.

CONVIVIALITY SHARE PRICE DROPS 60% AND TRADING SUSPENDED

Background: Conviviality, a listed company, was one of the UK's largest drinks wholesalers. It produced financial forecasts for the business and reported these to the stock market.

Error: In early 2018, Conviviality reported to the markets that profits would be 20% lower than the market expectation of £70 million, i.e., £14 million lower. While a large proportion of this shortfall was caused by weakened profit margins, it turned out that £5 million of the announced shortfall was caused by a 'material error in the financial forecasts' due to 'a spreadsheet arithmetic error'. On top of that, Conviviality also admitted that it had failed to budget for a tax payment of £30 million due at the end of the month.

Outcome: The share price dropped 60% before trading was suspended and the company was eventually sold.

Sources: http://www.eusprig.org/horror-stories.htm identifier POB1801

https://www.theguardian.com/business/2018/mar/21/bargain-booze-owner-conviviality-must-raise-125m-to-halt-bankruptcy

3. Learn from horror stories

https://www.accountingweb.co.uk/business/management-accounting/convivialitys-spreadsheet-hell-sinks-the-business

How to prevent such errors:

The press stories give us virtually no information about the spreadsheet error, saying only that it was an 'arithmetic error', so we can only imagine what might have been the cause. It may have been that an amount was subtracted when it should have been added or vice versa. This type of risk particularly arises if you always work with positive numbers. Then it is not always obvious whether to add or subtract them in calculations. For example, if you have a (positive) figure for 'net interest' or 'profit or loss on sale of asset' – does it represent income or a cost? This type of error can be avoided using a sign convention.

1. **Define and use a sign convention consistently:** We have covered this in the Fidelity story in chapter 3.2 'Incorrect inputs'. Show income and cash inflows as positive numbers, costs and cash outflows as negative numbers. Then you always add such numbers. You never have to decide if you must add or subtract a number in calculating profit or net cash flow. The risk of arithmetical error (such as adding instead of subtracting) is thus reduced.

2. **Understand mathematical operator precedence:** The mathematical operators such as + - * / as well as powers and brackets are commonly used in formulas. When calculating each formula, Excel does not simply work through it from left to right but applies the rules of precedence. Therefore, it is vital to understand them. One of the various acronyms can help you here. The version I learnt in the UK is BODMAS = Brackets, Order (power of), Division/Multiplication, Addition/Subtraction. This means that brackets are calculated first, followed by powers and so on. A simple example should help clarify the importance of such rules.

    The formula will be calculated following BODMAS: = 1 + 2 * 3 = 1 + 6 (multiplication has priority over addition, so 2 * 3 is calculated first) = 7

And not left to right (how some non-scientific calculators calculate): = 1 + 2 * 3 = 3 * 3 = 9

If you are unsure, or want to enforce another order or precedence, simply put brackets around suitable parts of your formula. Brackets (= B, the first letter in BODMAS) have the highest priority and are always calculated first. If you really wanted 1 + 2 to be calculated first in the above example, then you should write your formulas as = (1 + 2) * 3.

3. **Test and review your results:** If you follow the Golden Ground-rules and the tips above then the risk of errors is reduced but not eliminated. Therefore, suitable testing combined with a professional scepticism of results ('how can you be confident they are correct?') are vital. EuSpRig chairman Patrick O'Beirne says that such errors arise 'because people don't actually test their spreadsheets but accept an answer if it looks like what they expect or want.' Do not fall into that trap! Test your calculations and results. Use an assortment of possible inputs and also do plausibility reviews of the results: 'Does that make sense?' We cover this important topic in more detail in chapter 5 'Detect errors'.

3.5. COPY AND PASTE ERRORS

Copy and paste is very useful, easy to perform and commonly used… Ctrl C and Ctrl V are probably the most well-known Excel shortcuts. But this seemingly simple action can lead to expensive (but avoidable) errors, as the following examples show. These include (i) errors which were created during the copying and (ii) errors that were already in the cells being copied and were therefore repeated.

DOCTOR JOB OFFERS AND REJECTIONS SENT TO INCORRECT CANDIDATES

Background: The National Health Service in Britain used spreadsheets for assessing junior doctors' interview results.

Error: The spreadsheet with the results for each interview was copied into a new sheet with a different format and other errors were made, which resulted in incorrect rankings being assigned to interviewees.

Outcome: As a result, some job offers and rejections were sent to incorrect candidates. A statement by the British Medical Association said, 'There is no hiding from the fact that many trainees will have made huge life decisions based on their original offers.'

Source: http://www.nationalhealthexecutive.com/Health-Care-News/junior-doctor-jobs-offers-withdrawn-after-admin-blunder?dorewrite=false

How to prevent such errors:

This appears to be a case of errors arising during the copy-paste action, due to data becoming mixed up. You should therefore prevent this risk by avoiding copy-pasting where possible.

1. **Reduce the need for copy and paste actions:** Keep all your data (inputs), calculations and outputs in single file where possible. Inside this file, use lookup or SUMIF formulas or possibly pivot tables to perform calculations and produce your outputs, rather than copy-paste.

    If copy-paste actions are deemed necessary, however, then you should reduce the risk of error as follows, depending upon whether the areas you are copying contain primarily data or formulas.

Copying data

2. **Paste as values:** Generally, when copying data, you want to paste the data as values, even if they were calculations or linked cells in the section you copied. To do this, simply paste as values, as shown below. This is important as you do not want the formulas, which could create errors, in the new location or unnecessary links.

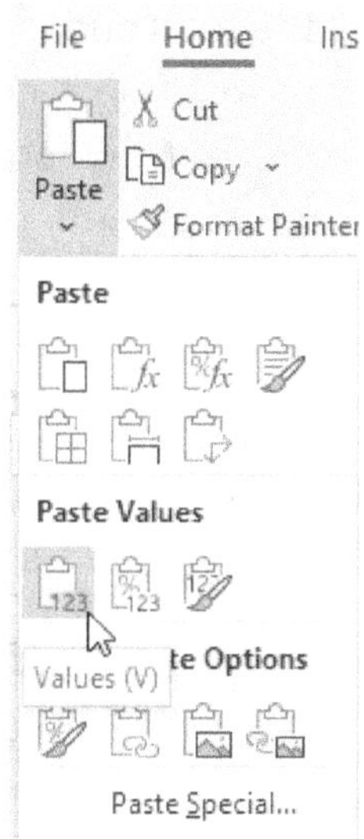

3. **Ensure source and destination areas have the same structure:** For example, if you are copying doctor names and results for 'Interview board 1' to a master list, you must ensure the doctor names are in the same order. To be honest, in this case you should use formulas to ensure you get the right results against the right names. If a number of source sheets must be completed e.g., by various interview boards, create and distribute a standard template for everyone to use. This should ensure that the columns and possibly the names (if known in advance) are in a consistent order.

4. **Consider protecting sheets to prevent changes:** You can protect any sheet from changes. This is useful if it contains data to be copied or pasted. This reduces the risk that a user changes the rows or columns and so creates a difference between the copy and paste areas, which could lead to errors when copying and pasting. See sub-chapter 2.4 'Rule #4 – Restrict access, inputs and changes' for details on sheet protection.

5. **Copy and paste the correct rows and columns:** This is best achieved using range names. Imagine we have two files: the first file contains the detailed planning of a marketing budget by brand for the coming year. We need to incorporate these costs in the main budget P&L file, but we do not want all the detailed marketing

budget calculations there, just the total budgeted costs per brand so we have decided to copy and paste the data into the main file. It is expected that we will have to repeat this action for the quarterly forecast updates. To ensure we copy and paste the correct data each time, I have set up a suitable range name in each file. For the marketing budget file, this range is on an output sheet and looks like the screenshot below.

	A	B
	Marketing_outputs	
	Name Box	
1	Marketing budget 20x1	
2		
3	Brand	Marketing (USD)
4	Alpha	10,000
5	Bravo	20,000
6	Charlie	12,000
7	Total	42,000

For the key data to be copied, I have defined a range name 'Marketing_outputs' by first selecting the relevant cells, then typing the desired name into the Name Box, above the Excel cells. This cannot contain any spaces, so use the underscore character if desired. To select this range in future, simply click on the down arrow in the Name Box and select the desired name.

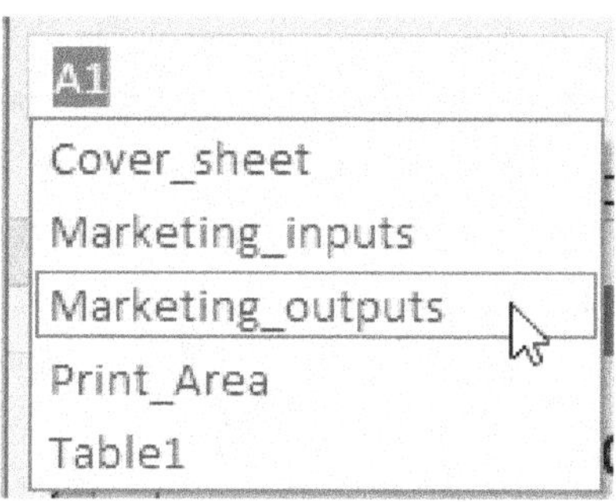

The predefined range is then automatically selected, no matter where you were in the file. Simply copy this data (e.g., using the shortcut Ctrl C) and then move to the second file, in our example this is the main P&L budget file. Here, we simply select the destination range name 'Marketing_inputs' and paste the data as values, as recommended above.

Marketing_inputs		
A	B	C
Marketing budget 20x1		
Brand	**Marketing (USD)**	
Alpha	10,000	
Bravo	20,000	
Charlie	12,000	
Total	**42,000**	
Check	-	[B8] =B7-SUM(B4:B6)

You may have noticed that I included the total line in the copied data. This is not 100% necessary, but it does allow me to add an extra check in the destination file (cell B8): does the copied total value equal the actual sum of the individual lines?

If the amount of data you are copy-pasting is quite large and/or comes from different parts of the source file, I recommend you set up a dedicated interface sheet in each file. This is a separate sheet in each file, especially for the purpose of doing the regular copy-paste action. For the source file, this is an output sheet and for the destination file, it is an input sheet. Apart from that, and the fact that the data ranges are larger, the process is the same as the simple example we just covered. I used such interface sheets for one client to copy IFRS 16 right-of-use assets plan values by entity from a detailed calculation file into the main planning file, where we did not want all the detailed calculations.

Copying formulas

6. **Correctly use cell reference fixing (anchoring):** Even if the original formulas being copied are free of error, new errors can be created by copying. This can arise if cell references in the copied cells have not been correctly fixed with dollar signs. Cell reference fixing is sometimes called anchoring. Whatever you call it, you need to be able to master this important Excel skill. To illustrate, I have created two examples of errors that can arise: one with missing cell-fixing and a second example with incorrect fixing.

i) **A formula needs fixing**

Background: Next to a P&L, a user wishes to calculate the percentage of sales for all lines. Such a 'common size' P&L is useful for comparisons e.g., of years or of divisions.

◢	A	B	C	D
1		TEUR	% Sales	[Cell] Formula
2	Sales	2,000		
3	Cost of sales	(1,200)	-60%	[C3] =B3/B2
4	**Gross Profit**	800	-67%	[C4] =B4/B3
5	Overheads	(400)	-50%	[C5] =B5/B4
6	**EBITDA**	400	-100%	[C6] =B6/B5
7	Depreciation	(150)	-38%	[C7] =B7/B6
8	**EBIT**	250	-167%	[C8] =B8/B7
9	Interest	(50)	-20%	[C9] =B9/B8
10	EBT	200	-400%	[C10] =B10/B9
11	Tax	(60)	-30%	[C11] =B11/B10
12	**Profit**	140	-233%	[C12] =B12/B11

Error: The user has entered the first formula for cost of sales in cell C3 which gives the correct result. He has then copied this formula down to the other rows.

Outcome: Unfortunately, the results for the other rows are incorrect since the denominator no longer refers to the sales row (row 2).

How to prevent such errors:

◢	A	B	C	D
1		TEUR	% Sales	[Cell] Formula
2	Sales	2,000	100%	[C2] =B2/B$2
3	Cost of sales	(1,200)	-60%	[C3] =B3/B$2
4	**Gross Profit**	800	40%	[C4] =B4/B$2
5	Overheads	(400)	-20%	[C5] =B5/B$2
6	**EBITDA**	400	20%	[C6] =B6/B$2
7	Depreciation	(150)	-8%	[C7] =B7/B$2
8	**EBIT**	250	13%	[C8] =B8/B$2
9	Interest	(50)	-3%	[C9] =B9/B$2
10	EBT	200	10%	[C10] =B10/B$2
11	Tax	(60)	-3%	[C11] =B11/B$2
12	**Profit**	140	7%	[C12] =B12/B$2

3. Learn from horror stories

The correct formula is shown above, with the row number 2 in the denominator fixed with a dollar sign. This formula can be copied to other rows and gives correct results in all cases because the dollar sign tells Excel not to change this part of the cell reference (in this case, the row 2) when the formula is copied. You can fix either the column only (dollar sign in front of the column letter), the row only as in our example (dollar sign in front of the row number) or both (dollar signs in front of both the column letter and the row number).

ii) A formula is fixed incorrectly

Fixing is often important, but you can have too much of a good thing as the following example shows.

Background: Here, a user wants to calculate the annual interest costs for two loans in each of five plan years. For each loan, we have the loan balance in each year, the interest rate for all periods and the calculated interest cost. Both loan calculations look, at first sight, to be consistent, which is best practice. So far, so good.

	A	B	C	D	E	F	G
1	USDk		Year 1	Year 2	Year 3	Year 4	Year 5
2							
3	**Loan 1**						
4	Loan balance		100	90	80	70	60
5	Interest rate p.a.	5.0%					
6	Interest cost		5	5	4	4	3
7	[Cell] Formula		[C6] =C4*$B$5	[D6] =D4*$B$5	[E6] =E4*$B$5	[F6] =F4*$B$5	[G6] =G4*$B$5
8							
9	**Loan 2**						
10	Loan balance		100	90	80	70	60
11	Interest rate p.a.	8.0%					
12	Interest cost		5	5	4	4	3
13	[Cell] Formula		[C12] =C10*$B$5	[D12] =D10*$B$5	[E12] =E10*$B$5	[F12] =F10*$B$5	[G12] =G10*$B$5

The interest cost formulas in row 6 (loan 1) and 12 (loan 2) refer to a cell containing the interest rate for each loan. Because the interest rate is in a single cell, the cell reference in the formula has been fixed with dollar signs in front of both column and row, so that when the formula is copied, the reference to the cell with the interest rate does not change. This is fine for loan 1.

Error: For the second loan, the user copies the whole calculation block for the first loan. In principle this is good practice and follows Golden Ground Rule #3, consistency of spreadsheet design. However, the second loan has a different interest rate. Since the reference to the cell with the interest rate was fixed for both row and column, the interest calculation in the second loan (row 12) incorrectly uses the interest rate for the first loan (cell B5).

Outcome: Consequently, the interest costs calculated for the second loan are incorrect and could result in too little funds being available to make interest payments or even a breach of covenants with associated restrictions or penalties.

How to prevent such errors:

	A	B	C	D	E	F	G
1	USDk		Year 1	Year 2	Year 3	Year 4	Year 5
2							
3	**Loan 1**						
4	Loan balance		100	90	80	70	60
5	Interest rate p.a.	5.0%					
6	Interest cost		5	5	4	4	3
7	[Cell] Formula		[C6] =C4*$B5	[D6] =D4*$B5	[E6] =E4*$B5	[F6] =F4*$B5	[G6] =G4*$B5
8							
9	**Loan 2**						
10	Loan balance		100	90	80	70	60
11	Interest rate p.a.	8.0%					
12	Interest cost		8	7	6	6	5
13	[Cell] Formula		[C12] =C10*$B11	[D12] =D10*$B11	[E12] =E10*$B11	[F12] =F10*$B11	[G12] =G10*$B11

The solution here relies on the fact that it is not necessary to fix both the row and the column of the cell containing the interest rate: it is only necessary to fix (have a dollar sign in front of) the column B in the formula. In this corrected version, the interest formulas for each loan refer to the interest rate cell for that loan (B5 or B11).

As a general rule for fixing: Fix as much as necessary but as little as possible. In the second example, it is only necessary to fix the column. And always review the results to identify any errors.

 **how2excel tip**

Use the F4 key to quickly fix cells

To easily fix a cell reference in a formula press F4 when the cursor is in or next to the relevant cell reference. This fixes (puts a dollar sign in front of) both row and column. Press F4 again to fix just the row. Press F4 again to fix just the column. Press F4 again to remove the fixing completely as the following example sequence shows.

A1 → $A$1 → A$1 → $A1 → A1

You can remember this order as follows: both, row, column, none. With practice, it becomes second nature to press F4 twice to fix the row only or three times to fix the column only.

COPY ERROR COSTS 16M POUNDS AND DELAYS THE OPENING OF A CHILDREN'S HOSPITAL

Background: The construction of a new children's hospital in Scotland was put out to tender. The hospital plan included care rooms where the air needs to be changed 10 times per hour to help reduce the risk of infections.

Error: Relevant data for the construction formed part of the documents sent out to potential bidders. The care rooms' data was included in a spreadsheet called 'the environmental matrix'. Unfortunately, the required number of hourly air changes was entered as four, not ten. A report into the matter by Grant Thornton states: 'This looks to be, based on our review, human error in copying across the ... generic ventilation criteria into the critical care room detail'.

A second error in the environmental matrix concerning the requirement for areas of critical care to have en suite bathrooms was picked up in a review and corrected, but not the care room ventilation error. The whole project was sent out to tender, and the tender documents therefore included the requirement for four not ten air changes per hour in the care rooms. Although the error was picked up by one bidder, and corrected in their bid, they did not win the contract and since the correction was not noticed during the bid review, it was not notified to other bidders. The winning bidder then installed care room ventilation to comply with the lower figure of four air changes per hour.

Outcome: This error had not only had a financial impact – the air change equipment had to be replaced at an additional cost of 16m pounds – but it also had an impact on sick children, because it also delayed the opening of the hospital while the remedial work was carried out.

Source: https://www.bbc.com/news/uk-scotland-edinburgh-east-fife-53893101

How to prevent such errors:

Check any data in sections copy-pasted from somewhere else: This case reaffirms the need to check and validate your data. Although it is best practice to re-use calculations (test once, use many times), you have to be careful to ensure that you make any necessary changes for differences between the two calculations. This is often the case for input data, as we can see here. Another example would be a sales calculation for company A with a planned sales growth rate of 6% p.a. copied to company B where the rate should only be 2% p.a. The calculation logic may be valid, but if the inputs are not updated as necessary, garbage in leads to garbage out (the GIGO concept).

Please refer to sub-chapter 3.2 'Incorrect inputs' for more detailed advice.

Not only have 'copy and paste' actions caused errors. Its sibling 'cut and paste' has also caused havoc.

TRANSALTA CUT & PASTE ERROR COSTS OVER $24 MILLION

Background: TransAlta, a big Canadian power generator was buying power transmission hedging contracts, which it assessed using a spreadsheet.

Error: Reuters quotes the Chief Executive Steve Snyder explaining that it was 'literally a cut-and-paste error in an Excel spreadsheet that we did not detect when we did our final sorting and ranking bids prior to submission.'

Outcome: The mistake led to TransAlta buying power at higher prices than it should have, which cost it over $24 million.

Source:
https://www.theregister.co.uk/2003/06/19/excel_snafu_costs_firm_24m/

How to prevent such errors:

Cut and paste actions do not generally cause errors of the kind described above for copy and paste because the cell references are not changed. Perhaps individual rows of contract data were cut and pasted into a new order of e.g., from cheapest to most expensive. Especially if columns or rows of data are hidden (which is itself not best practice), data can get scrambled such that the data in some columns (e.g., contracts A, B, C) no longer match to data in other columns (e.g., contracts C, A, B).

Such a cut and paste action is both error-prone and inefficient and there are better ways of achieving the desired result using standard Excel functionality as follows.

1. **Do not use hidden rows or columns:** These can be easily overlooked when copy & pasting, cut & pasting and analysing. If necessary, use groupings instead so that there is a clear indication that there is unseen content.

	A	B	E	G
1	Contract	Base price	Date rec'd	
2	Armstrong	10,000	1/2/20x2	
3	Aldrin	12,000	22/2/20x2	
4	Collins	9,500	12/3/20x2	

In the screenshot above, columns C and D contain important data but have been hidden. This is not obvious at first glance. Cutting and pasting data in columns A and B will mismatch this data with the hidden data in columns C and D. If you must 'hide' certain rows or columns, please use groupings, such as for column F in the above example. These are more obvious as there is a plus symbol above relevant columns (here, above column G), or to the left of relevant rows, for row groupings.

2. **Use sort functionality:** Assuming that the data for each contract under consideration is in a single row (often the best design), use the 'sort' function to sort all the data e.g., from cheapest to most expensive; do not manually cut and paste as this is both time-consuming and error-prone. You can also leave your source data unchanged and create a sorted version using dynamic arrays (see point 5).

3. **Use filters:** If the data for each contract under consideration is not in a single row, for example because calculations are required that are spread over several rows (possibly a sub-optimal design), then sorting is not an option. Instead, you can filter the list to show e.g., the three contracts with the lowest costs: 'Cost' column filter, Number filters, Top 10..., Bottom 3 items

3. Learn from horror stories

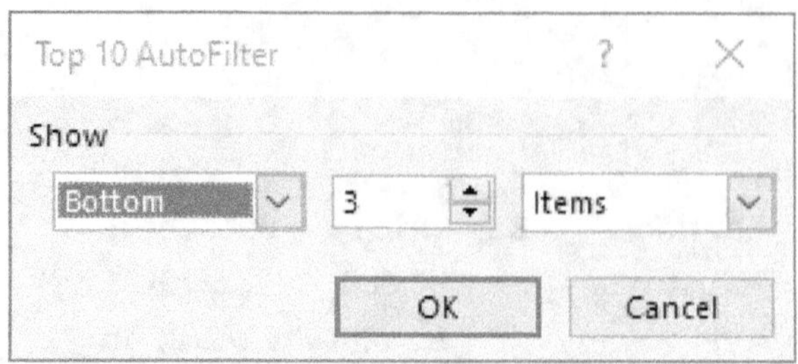

▲	A	B
1	Contrac ▼	Cost ▼
4	C	29
5	D	62
8	G	40

4. **Use ranks:** Alternatively, you can use the RANK.EQ function. This lets you see the rank in the complete list, as shown below.

▲	A	B	C	D
1	Contrac ▼	Cost ▼	Rank ▼	[Cell] Formula ▼
2	A	71	5	[C2] =RANK.EQ(B2,$B$2:$B$9,1)
3	B	100	8	[C3] =RANK.EQ(B3,$B$2:$B$9,1)
4	C	29	1	[C4] =RANK.EQ(B4,$B$2:$B$9,1)
5	D	62	3	[C5] =RANK.EQ(B5,$B$2:$B$9,1)
6	E	96	7	[C6] =RANK.EQ(B6,$B$2:$B$9,1)
7	F	68	4	[C7] =RANK.EQ(B7,$B$2:$B$9,1)
8	G	40	2	[C8] =RANK.EQ(B8,$B$2:$B$9,1)
9	H	81	6	[C9] =RANK.EQ(B9,$B$2:$B$9,1)

The 1 at the end of the formula indicates ascending values i.e., low values are best. Use 0 for descending values i.e., high values are best. If the list is long, you can then filter the list to show e only ranks 1 to 3, for example, which gives the same results as filter top 3, only now you can see at a glance the ranking – useful when filtering a higher number of top X items.

5. **Use dynamic array functions:** If you have Office 365, you can use the new dynamic arrays functions such as SORT, FILTER and UNIQUE

to create automatic output lists from your data. For example, use the function SORT and complete the arguments to define the array to be sorted, the row or column to sort by, the sort order (ascending or descending) and if you want to sort by row or column. Dynamic array functions can help you avoid manually processing or changing (e.g. filtering or sorting) your source data and so can help you avoid some of the errors that can occur. As with all Excel functions that you use, learn to use them correctly and always check your results.

LONDON WHALE CASE COSTS JP MORGAN OVER $6 BILLION

Background: JP Morgan used a spreadsheet model to determine and assess value at risk (VAR) for its credit portfolio. This comprised a number of files and as part of the process for using the VAR model, a user had to copy and paste model content from one spreadsheet to another. Although the spreadsheet went through a review process, some reports indicate that the review team was under time pressure and approved the model despite the inefficient and potentially risky copy-paste process.

Error: The case is large and complicated (see YouTube for detailed videos), and the use of spreadsheets is only part of the story. Apparently, the copied cells contained various mathematical errors, including using the sum of two numbers instead of the average in calculating volatility. These errors were not detected or corrected, and the copied cells repeated and perpetuated these errors.

Outcome: JP Morgan significantly underestimated its credit portfolio risk. There were accusations of fraud and a cover-up, with expensive lawsuits filed by investors. A 129-page report into the matter described the risk model as 'error-prone'. The case reportedly cost JP Morgan over $6 billion in losses and fines.

Sources: https://www.bloomberg.com/quicktake/the-london-whale

https://www.businessinsider.com/excel-partly-to-blame-for-trading-loss-2013-2?r=DE&IR=T

How to prevent such errors:

For the sake of clarity, we are interested here only in the spreadsheet errors. What you need to do is prevent (or detect and correct) errors before copying. Because if the copied cells contain errors, these will be copied and duplicated. This was the case in London Whale, where they apparently ended up with errors in all their VAR calculations!

1. **Use the Warren Buffet rule of modelling:** Warren Buffet's famous rule of investing is 'only invest in what you understand'. I have amended this to create the equivalent Warren Buffet rule of modelling:

   'Only model what you understand.'

   In this case, the subject (VAR) is technical, and you should only attempt to model it if you really understand it. Alternatively, do the modelling with an expert who can explain the calculations needed and act as a second set of eyes. In this way, you can hopefully avoid the kind of error that occurred here: adding instead of averaging two numbers.

2. **Test your calculations**: Especially if a section is to be copied, test it thoroughly to be as sure as you can that it is free of material error. In cases like this, where the calculation is both technical and critical – the VAR for a credit portfolio – you can test the calculation using predefined test cases: inputs with known or expected results that can be run though the Excel calculation to check if the results produced materially agree to the test case results. In addition, a review by an expert can help uncover errors and generally improve the reliability of calculations by challenging calculation logic and assumptions.

We cover testing in more detail in sub-chapter 5.2 'Review and test your spreadsheet'. For now, let us move on to the next collection of horror stories.

3.6. Incorrect links

I have reviewed many models in my time and found that incorrect links, especially links to other worksheets or even other workbooks, are a common cause of errors. Because the linked cells are, by definition, on another sheet, it is not always easy to spot an error. But the goods news here is: follow best practice and you can reduce the risk of error considerably. You can also make your model easier to understand and to use; what more could you possibly want?

INCORRECT LINK CAUSES $6 MILLION ERROR

Background: Knox County in Tennessee, USA used a spreadsheet to report data to auditors, including bank account balances.

Error: In the list of bank balances, one account was incorrectly linked.

Outcome: As a result, the total of all the bank balances reported to the auditors was understated by over $6 million.

Source: https://www.quickbase.com/blog/spreadsheet-horror-stories

How to prevent such errors:

You can use the following tips and tricks to help ensure you link to the correct column and row on another sheet.

1. **Follow Golden Ground Rule #2 – Keep your worksheets as clear and simple as possible:** Similar to copying linked cell formulas across rows, copying such formulas down a column can also create errors if the content or row order on the two sheets differs. In cases like this, some Excel users like to use VLOOKUP or INDEX and MATCH to get the data they want and at the same time avoid incorrect linking. This can be a useful approach, but it is not one I prefer for the following reasons:

   a) The formulas are more complicated than a simple link, which is all that is needed. This increases the risk of error and contravenes Golden Ground Rule #2: Keep your worksheets as clear and simple as possible.

b) VLOOKUP suffers from a number of disadvantages which I explain in chapter 4 'Avoid common function errors'.

c) I prefer direct links where possible as these make it easier for model testing – see chapter 6 'Find and correct errors' for more details.

2. **Follow Golden Ground Rule #3 – Use a clear, clean, consistent design:** One cause of such errors is inconsistent columns (usually periods such as years) on the linked sheets. For example, let us say that you create a link for the first period in your model from a calculation sheet to an input sheet, which is correct, and then copy this across to all the other periods in further columns. If the period structure of the two sheets is inconsistent, then the links will be incorrect. To avoid this kind of error (as well as some copy-paste errors), and to generally make working with the model easier, ensure that the period structure of the columns is consistent across all data sheets e.g., year 2021 is in column C and increases by one year in each further column on all sheets. No half-years or quarters or comments etc. should be inserted in the middle of the annual periods on any sheet. This should help ensure that you link to the correct columns when copying formulas across an entire row.

3. **Add checks:** If you are creating many links e.g., from a calculations sheet to an input sheet you can calculate the total of the values on each sheet and then check that these two totals agree.

	A	B	C	D
1			Balance GBPk	
2	Account number	Bank	31.12.20xx	[Cell] Formula
3				
4	12345678	Big Bank	4,567,891	[C4] ='Bank balance data'!C3
5	45612378	Regional Bank	561,851	[C5] ='Bank balance data'!C4
6	78912345	Local Bank	-	[C6] ='Bank balance data'!C7
7		Total	5,129,742	[C7] =SUM(C4:C6)
8		Check	(691,076)	[C8] =C7-'Bank balance data'!C6

The example shown above uses bank balances, as in the Knox County story. Each row shows a bank account number, the bank's name and the balance. The balance for the Local Bank account in row 6 has been incorrectly linked to cell C7 instead of C5 on the source sheet. This error may not be obvious as the bank may actually have a nil balance, or the falsely linked-to cell may contain a number representing something completely different. Either way, you have an error.

To detect this type of error, there is a total formula as well as a check. With this "total" check, you can clearly see there is an error, as the total of the linked cells does not equal the total of the input sheet cells. You can then investigate and resolve.

This tip is particularly useful if your source data is not in a block of rows, one after the after as above, but spread out over an entire sheet. For example, in financial models I often have P&L and balance sheet values for actual periods (inputs) that then flow via value driver sheets (calculations) into the financial statement sheets (outputs). If all works correctly, the P&L and balance sheet totals in actual periods in the output sheets should agree to the totals in the input sheets, because we do not change actual data (we only use them as a basis for plan periods). Therefore, I add checks to ensure that this is so.

We will cover the important topic of checks in more detail in sub-chapter 5.1 'Build in error checks and a master check'.

---

how2excel tip

Use formulas for labels

	A	B	C	D
1			Balance GBPk	
2	Account number	Bank	31.12.20xx	[Cell] Formula
3				
4	12345678	Big Bank	4,567,891	[B4] ='Bank balance data'!B3
5	45612378	Regional Bank	561,851	[B5] ='Bank balance data'!B4
6	0		0	-	[B6] ='Bank balance data'!B7
7		Total	5,129,742	[C7] =SUM(C4:C6)

> Here we have the same example as above. In this case, I have copied the linked formulas for values from column C into columns A and B where the account numbers and bank names should appear. Here the error becomes obvious due to the zeros which appear and can be corrected. Once you have correctly linked the formulas in row 6 (e.g., by copying down the formulas from row 5), the correct details will appear in columns A and B.

If you combine this tip with the "Totals" check above, then you really have a belt and braces approach which should really ensure no link errors: The total check **detects** any error, and the label links help you **find and correct** it.

4. **Avoid links to external files:** Such links can be treacherous to keep correctly updated and they can represent a black box which impedes transparency and increases the risk of error. Especially here, it is essential to ensure consistent column structure between source and destination files, as noted above. This can be hard to ensure, and errors can easily arise e.g., if a user of the source data spreadsheet inserts a new column or row when the destination file is closed, then the links are not automatically updated as they are when everything is in a single file. Therefore, if sheets in external files are essential to your spreadsheet, consider moving them into the main file by using the move command: right-click on the worksheet tab of the sheet to be moved, select 'Move or copy', under 'To book' select the main spreadsheet and relevant sheet location and click 'Ok'. If the moved sheets contain links to the source file, you may wish to review and remove these using 'Data', 'Edit Links'.

Note: As noted before, removing links to external files can be a challenge so I have written a blog on the subject to help you: https://www.how2excel.com/en/get-rid-of-those-annoying-links/

3.7. CIRCULAR ERRORS AND MISTAKES IN LOGIC

These kinds of error can be tricky to avoid and troublesome to find. But by now I hope you have built up your confidence: where there is a will and friendly Excel advice to help you, there is a way. This way, please...

FUNDING SHORTFALL CAUSED BY CIRCULAR REFERENCE ERROR

Background: A large client had a five-year planning model including long-term debts and an overdraft facility. Interest was calculated on these debts as the average of the opening and closing balance for the year multiplied by the relevant interest rate p.a. These interest costs created the need for extra financing, which increased the interest cost, which... sent the calculation around in circles. This is what is known as a circular reference. I call it a logical circular reference (i) because it arises due to the logic of the calculation and (ii) to distinguish it from an erroneous circular reference. In this case, the logical circular reference was intentional, and this technique is quite common in debt modelling.

Error: In addition to the intentional circular references, there was also an unintentional and erroneous circular reference in the model which led to sales being overstated. This error was not identified because the client had turned on iterations to avoid Excel reporting the logical circular reference (see below for details of this option).

Outcome: The overstatement of sales caused a shortage of funding, which delayed an important investment in new machinery for a planned expansion.

Source: Author's own experience.

How to prevent such errors:

First, we should take a closer look at circular references to understand them better before we can tackle the topic of how best to deal with them and avoid errors.

1. **Recognise when you have one:** This is easy as Excel gives you a warning like this.

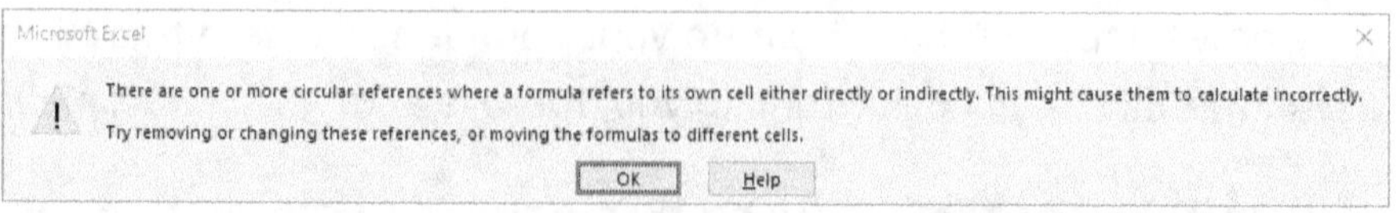

Note that the message is a warning (the icon is an exclamation mark) not an error as the circular references may be intentional (which we cover below). Excel also tries to mark the first circular reference loop it finds with blue precedent/dependent lines, which can be very helpful.

2. **Understand the two types of circular references:**

As indicated in the story above, I group circular references into two categories: erroneous and logical.

a. **Erroneous circular references**

The easiest example is when a SUM formula includes the cell containing the SUM formula itself, as shown in the screenshot below for a fruit seller. Column A shows the type of fruit sold, column B shows the number of units sold and at the end we have a total. The total is zero, which cannot be correct and so is clearly an error.

	A	B	C
1	Fruit	Units sold	[Cell] Formula
2	Apples	10	
3	Bananas	20	
4	Cherries	30	
5	Total	-	[B5] =SUM(B2:B5)

More importantly, Excel gives you the circularity warning message but, in this case, it is not able to mark the related cells with blue lines since it all happens on a single cell (B5). Since you get the warning message that there is a circular reference as soon as it is created, you know that what you just did was the cause. Have a look and fix the error. In this case, the cause and solution are easy to find. Change the SUM formula in cell B5 to exclude cell B5 itself. In other cases, you may need to search for longer to find and understand the entire loop, particularly if this covers several worksheets. In this case, you may use the auditing toolbar in the Formulas ribbon to trace them.

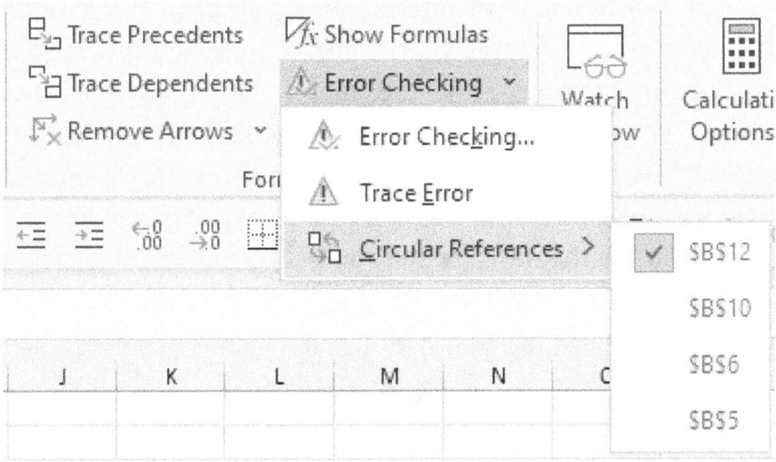

b. Logical circular references

In the example below, Excel has helpfully and automatically marked the first circular reference loop it has found with blue precedent/dependent lines.

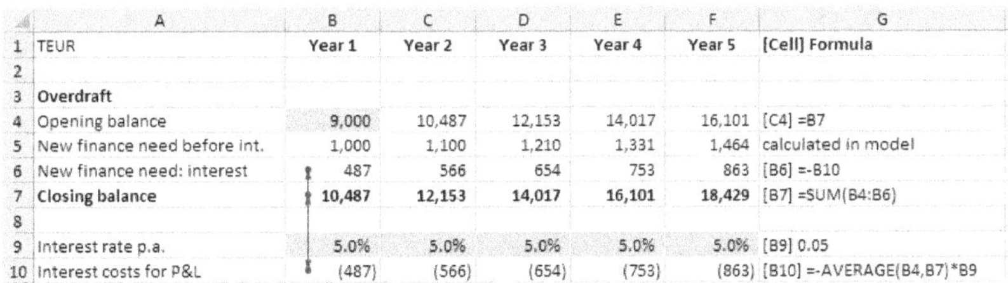

	A	B	C	D	E	F	G
1	TEUR	Year 1	Year 2	Year 3	Year 4	Year 5	[Cell] Formula
2							
3	Overdraft						
4	Opening balance	9,000	10,487	12,153	14,017	16,101	[C4] =B7
5	New finance need before int.	1,000	1,100	1,210	1,331	1,464	calculated in model
6	New finance need: interest	487	566	654	753	863	[B6] =-B10
7	Closing balance	10,487	12,153	14,017	16,101	18,429	[B7] =SUM(B4:B6)
8							
9	Interest rate p.a.	5.0%	5.0%	5.0%	5.0%	5.0%	[B9] 0.05
10	Interest costs for P&L	(487)	(566)	(654)	(753)	(863)	[B10] =-AVERAGE(B4,B7)*B9

Here, the user wants to calculate the necessary overdraft balance in each of five years. This includes financing needs calculated elsewhere in the model (row 5) plus interest on the overdraft itself (row 6). These interest costs are taken from row 10, where they are calculated based upon the average of the opening and closing overdraft balances. Since the closing balance includes the interest on the closing balance, we have a circular reference loop.

A logical circular reference does not arise in reality with your bank, so why can it arise in a model? The answer is that in real life, the bank can calculate the interest on a daily basis based upon the opening balance of each day. In a model, however, the periods are often years or months, and the balance can change significantly during such periods. Therefore, many spreadsheet users prefer to use the 'average balance approach' quoted in this example and argue that it is more accurate than using (say) the opening balance of the period as the basis for the interest calculation. We will look at this argument in just a minute. But first, let us look at practical matters.

3. **Understand the two common approaches to address circular references:**

There are two methods generally used to deal with circular references: (i) using iterations and (ii) using a copy-paste macro. Let us look at these two methods in turn and then (iii) assess what is best.

Method 1: Using iterations

Nature abhors a vacuum and Excel abhors a circular reference and it tells you so in no uncertain terms when you create one in your model... unless you turn on iterations, which the client in question had done. You will find this option under 'File', 'Excel Options' as shown in the screenshot below.

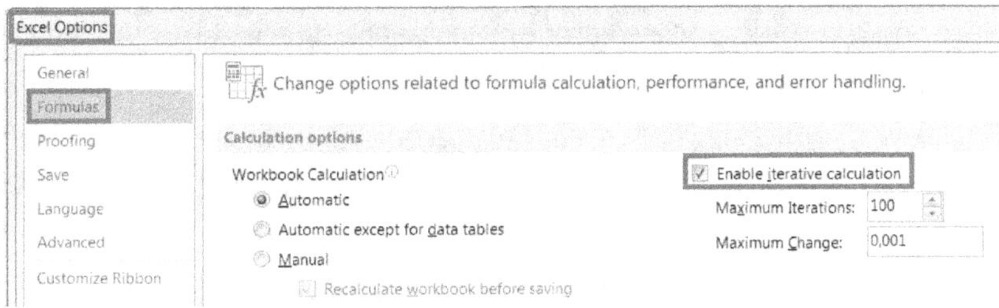

That is the first way of dealing with a logical circular reference and it has many fans because it is easy (simply turn on iterations), and the interest is calculated 'accurately'. Unfortunately, circular references with iterations turned on have some disadvantages:

- They make models more difficult to understand and sometimes also to operate e.g., using goal seek or data tables.

- They can hide unwanted and erroneous circular references, as in the above story.

- The interest figures may not necessarily be more accurate, as we will see below.

Method 2: Using a macro

The second way of dealing with circular references is to create a copy-paste macro that breaks the circular flow in the model by copying and pasting relevant data.

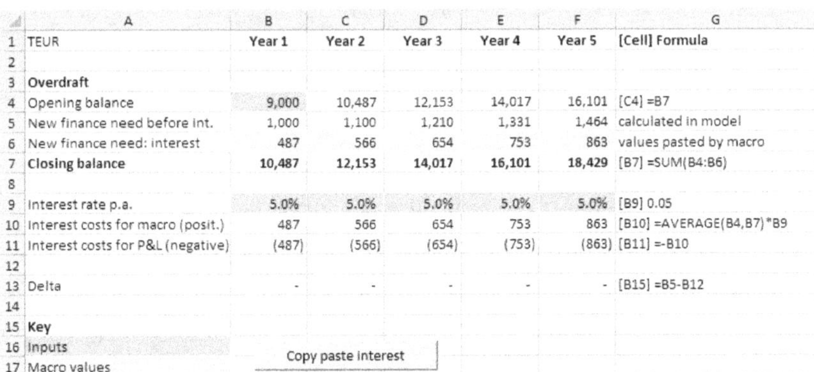

	A	B	C	D	E	F	G
1	TEUR	Year 1	Year 2	Year 3	Year 4	Year 5	[Cell] Formula
2							
3	Overdraft						
4	Opening balance	9,000	10,487	12,153	14,017	16,101	[C4] =B7
5	New finance need before int.	1,000	1,100	1,210	1,331	1,464	calculated in model
6	New finance need: interest	487	566	654	753	863	values pasted by macro
7	Closing balance	10,487	12,153	14,017	16,101	18,429	[B7] =SUM(B4:B6)
8							
9	Interest rate p.a.	5.0%	5.0%	5.0%	5.0%	5.0%	[B9] 0.05
10	Interest costs for macro (posit.)	487	566	654	753	863	[B10] =AVERAGE(B4,B7)*B9
11	Interest costs for P&L (negative)	(487)	(566)	(654)	(753)	(863)	[B11] =-B10
12							
13	Delta	-	-	-	-	-	[B15] =B5-B12
14							
15	Key						
16	Inputs						
17	Macro values						

In the example shown above, the macro (started by clicking the grey button 'Copy paste interest') copies the calculated data in row 10 to row 6, which is marked in light green to indicate that the cells are pasted there by the macro. It does this 20 times to ensure that the deltas (differences) between the two rows (shown in row 13) disappear i.e., become zero. The results are identical with the first method. This should be no surprise because the macro effectively replicates the iteration performed by Excel.

This technique also has its fans, maybe because they like clicking macro buttons! It has the advantage that because it is restricted to one circular reference, it cannot hide other, unwanted and erroneous circular references. But the solution still has disadvantages:

- It is a 'black box' for those unfamiliar with macros.

- The macro can contain errors that are not visible as errors in the spreadsheet itself and so are more likely to go undetected.

- It does not remove the circular reference but simply controls it.

- It may not be obvious to users that data in the model is not up-to-date if the macro has not been run since the last model changes.

- You cannot use this solution with goal seek or data tables.

- Lastly, as we will see below, the resulting interest figures may not necessarily be accurate anyway.

4. **Avoid circular references:**

Both of the above solutions for circular references have disadvantages; therefore, I personally prefer to calculate interest based upon the opening balance plus drawdowns (increases) or upon the average of opening balance and closing balance *before interest*. Some people object to this approach because the interest figures are then 'not accurate'. But my response is as follows:

a. For some loans, any increase (e.g., drawdown of a new loan) may well be at the start of a period and repayments may well be at the end of the period. In such cases, it is more accurate to use the opening balance for the calculation as this represents the outstanding balance for the whole period. Using the average of opening and closing as a basis for the interest calculation would be wrong here.

b. Even where that is not the case, e.g., a revolver (overdraft) facility, we must remember that a planning model is only an approximate depiction of reality and actual results will always differ to plan figures.

c. The difference between interest figures calculated using average balance and opening balance is often not material, as the example below shows.

	A	B	C	D	E	F	G
1	TEUR	Year 1	Year 2	Year 3	Year 4	Year 5	[Cell] Formula
2							
3	Overdraft						
4	Opening balance	9,000	10,500	12,180	14,060	16,160	[C4] =B7
5	New finance need before int.	1,000	1,100	1,210	1,331	1,464	calculated in model
6	New finance need: interest	500	580	670	770	881	[B6] =-B10
7	Closing balance	10,500	12,180	14,060	16,160	18,505	[B7] =SUM(B4:B6)
8							
9	Interest rate p.a.	5.0%	5.0%	5.0%	5.0%	5.0%	[B9] 0.05
10	Interest costs for P&L	(500)	(580)	(670)	(770)	(881)	[B10] =-SUM(B4:B5)*B9
11							
12	Comparison with average balance method						
13	Interest cost (ave. bal.)	(487)	(566)	(654)	(753)	(863)	
14	Delta	(13)	(14)	(15)	(17)	(18)	[B14] =B10-B13
15	Delta as % interest (ave. bal.)	2.6%	2.5%	2.3%	2.2%	2.1%	[B15] =B$14/B13
16	Delta as % closing balance	-0.1%	-0.1%	-0.1%	-0.1%	-0.1%	[B16] =B$14/B7

Here I have calculated the interest based upon the sum of the opening balance and the new financing need before interest. I have not included the interest in order to avoid a circular reference. Below, I have compared the results to the interest figures based upon the average balance's interest calculation (with circular reference and iterations turned on). In this example, the difference (delta) is small and in my opinion acceptable in a planning model. The advantages of avoiding circular references completely are (i) clear calculations without iteration or macro, (ii) no hiding of any potentially unwanted and erroneous circular references that may arise, (iii) you can also use goal seek and data tables if necessary. I rest my case!

WEST COAST FRANCHISE ERRORS COST AN ESTIMATED £49 MILLION

Background: In 2012, the UK Government's Department of Transport ran a bidding process to decide who would operate the West Coast Main Line. This comprised major train routes and represented a five-billion-pound franchise. Bids were received from both First Group and Virgin Trains, the franchise operator at that time. A financial model spreadsheet formed a key part of the process to assess the rival bids.

Error: There were numerous issues with the whole bidding process, highlighted later by a public enquiry and detailed in the Laidlaw Report (Laidlaw, 2012). 'Senior management did not have proper oversight of the project. Cuts in staffing and in consultancy budgets contributed to a lack of key skills.' In addition, 'consultants discover[ed] that the spreadsheet on which all calculations were modelled was fundamentally flawed. The key mechanism, called the GDP resilience model, mixed up real and inflated financial figures and contained elements of double counting.'

Outcome: The franchise was initially awarded to First Group, but Virgin Trains launched a legal challenge against the decision, which triggered an enquiry and eventually led to the franchise finally being re-awarded to Virgin Trains, the existing operator. The National Audit Office concluded that there was a 'significant cost to the taxpayer' including an estimated £40 million compensation to the bidders as well as £9 million of costs for staff, advisers, lawyers and two reviews into the whole affair.

Sources: https://www.bbc.com/news/uk-politics-21577826

https://www.theguardian.com/politics/2012/oct/05/west-coast-civil-servant-transport

How to prevent such errors:

The reports mentioned two significant errors in the spreadsheet model used: (i) mixing up real and inflated (nominal) figures and (ii) double counting. Let us look how to prevent these errors in turn.

Mixing up real and nominal figures

---

1. **Understand the terms real and nominal:**

   Real numbers are values in which any inflation effect has been stripped out. Such numbers can be useful in economics to better assess economic trends for numbers such as GDP, personal income, or interest rates. If you are earning 1% p.a. interest on your savings but inflation is running at 3% p.a. you can see that the real interest rate is negative (approximately -2%) - your savings are losing purchasing power.

   Nominal numbers are the amounts that include the effects of inflation and represent what you actually pay or receive (or plan to). These are typically the numbers we want to use in planning spreadsheets. For example, it is no good planning that the real cost of staff next year will be the same as this year because you expect to give them a pay rise equal to inflation. The plan costs must include the inflationary pay rise because that is what you will pay.

2. **As a general rule, always use nominal figures:** Include total expected changes (including real and inflationary rises) in all financial numbers being modelled including sales, costs, capex and working capital. This will better reflect reality because nominal amounts represent what you (plan to) actually pay, and these are also the correct basis to use for discounted cash flows.

   Note: Please see the free bonus file available at https://www.knott-consulting.com/en/book/ for an example of how to calculate plan values using percentage price changes as inputs.

3. **Never do calculations in output sheets other than plus/minus, SUM and possibly simple KPIs:** In one case, I saw a spreadsheet

where real figures were calculated and then passed to the P&L account (outputs sheet), where they were increased for inflation (calculations) in the individual P&L account lines using links to both the real numbers in the main calculations sheet and to inflation percentage increase figures in the assumptions sheet. I do not recommend this approach because (i) it mixed calculations and outputs, which should be kept separate for clarity and (ii) I could not easily check the calculations because each one was in a single line and contained links to two other sheets. Instead, calculate nominal values clearly on a calculation sheet and spread them over a suitable number of rows for clarity. (The download file referred to in point 2 above gives an example). Then simply link the calculated figures to the financial statements or other output sheets.

We now move onto double counting which I have split into double counting with formulas and double counting with cell linkages.

Double counting with formulas

---

1. Understand how double counting with formulas can occur:

	A	B	C
1	Calculations - Costs	CADk	[Cell] Formula
2			
3	General and admin.		
4	General	(100)	
5	Admin	(50)	
6	General and admin.	(150)	[B6] =SUM(B4:B5)
7			
8	Sales and distribution		
9	Sales	(35)	
10	Distribution	(65)	
11	Sales and distribution	(100)	[B11] =SUM(B9:B10)
12			
13	Total costs (incorrect)	(400)	[B13] =SUM(B4:B10)
14	Total costs (correct)	(250)	[B14] =B6+B11

In the simple example shown above, subtotals have been calculated using SUM and one of these has been incorrectly included in the total costs SUM formula in cell B13.

Note: The blue box and lines in the screenshot above were easily created using the auditing toolbar in Excel. This is covered in more detail in sub-chapter 6.1 'Standard Excel'.

2. **Only add up subtotals:** See the correct formula in cell B14.

3. **Only use the SUBTOTAL function with caution:** An alternative solution to the above double counting error is to use the function SUBTOTAL since this ignores other SUBTOTAL results.

	A	B	C
1	Calculations - Costs	CADk	[Cell] Formula
2			
3	**General and admin.**		
4	General	(100)	
5	Admin	(50)	
6	General and admin.	(150)	[B6] =SUBTOTAL(9,B4:B5)
7			
8	**Sales and distribution**		
9	Sales	(35)	
10	Distribution	(65)	
11	Sales and distribution	(100)	[B11] =SUBTOTAL(9,B9:B10)
12			
13	**Total costs**	(250)	[B13] =SUBTOTAL(9,B4:B12)

If filters are in use, the SUBTOTAL function also ignores data that is not visible. This feature makes it very useful when analysing data but if a total flows further in your workbook, this is risky as the total may not always be correct, as the following screenshot – with a filter in use – shows.

▲	A	B	C
1	Calculations - Costs ⊽	CADk ▽	[Cell] Formula ▽
2			
3	**General and admin.**		
4	General	(100)	
6	General and admin.	(100)	[B6] =SUBTOTAL(9,B4:B5)
7			
8	**Sales and distribution**		
9	Sales	(35)	
11	Sales and distribution	(35)	[B11] =SUBTOTAL(9,B9:B10)
12			
13	**Total costs**	(135)	[B13] =SUBTOTAL(9,B4:B12)

Totals costs are shown as 135 CADk as this represents only the visible rows. If this cell is linked onwards in the workbook, this probably represents an error. Solution: If (as in this example) you are not performing data analysis, then ignore SUBTOTAL and (correctly) calculate totals using SUM or +.

 **how2excel tip**

Calculate SUM and SUBTOTAL for key data columns

If you are performing data analysis and want to use filters and SUBTOTALS, then the solution I use is to calculate both SUM and SUBTOTALS for key data columns in two separate rows, usually above the data columns for ease of reference. The SUM result showing the total of all amounts in the column is then always visible and can be linked onwards in the workbook (if necessary) and the SUBTOTAL can be used for filtering and data analysis. If no filters are set, the two formulas should give the same result.

1. Understand how double counting with cell linkages can occur:

	A	B	C	D	E	F
1	Calculations - Costs	CADk			Outputs - P&L account	CADk
2						
3	General and admin.				xxx	
4	General	(100)			xxx	
5	Admin	(50)			Sales and distribution	(100)
6	General and admin.	(150)			General and admin.	(250)
7					Total costs	(350)
8	Sales and distribution				xxx	
9	Sales	(35)			xxx	
10	Distribution	(65)				
11	Sales and distribution	(100)				
12						
13	Total costs	(250)			Check	(100)
14	[Cell] Formula	[B13] =B6+B11				[F13] =F7-B13

In the new screenshot above, the total costs formula in the calculations block on the left is now correct. In the P&L outputs on the right (which would usually be on a separate sheet), the costs have been linked to the calculations block on the left. Unfortunately, the General & Administration (G&A) costs have been incorrectly linked to the total costs of 250 CADk and not to the total G&A costs of 150 CADk. The result is that the Sales & Distribution (S&D) costs of 100 CADk are double counted: once in the S&D figure (correct) and again in the G&A figure (incorrect).

2. Calculate figures for the outputs in the same order as the outputs:

This is another example of Golden Ground Rule # 3 – put simply, consistency is key. On my value driver worksheets, I calculate values for each position in the financial statements (P&L and balance sheet) in exactly the same order as these positions appear in the financial statement outputs: I start with P&L positions – first sales, then costs and tax – and follow these with balance sheet positions – first assets and then equity and liabilities.

In the example above, this rule was not followed: calculations are in the order G&A followed by S&D, but the outputs show them the other way around. This may have led to the error: S&D output is linked to S&D calculation; the next output item (G&A) is linked to the next calculation item, but this is 'Total costs' not 'G&A costs.'

3. **If you break this rule, only do so for a valid reason and make it clear**: Simply include a title at the relevant position on the calculation sheet and say where the actual calculation can be found. In my models this is typically the case for two P&L positions that are related to balance sheet positions, and I prefer to keep the calculations together:

    - Depreciation and amortisation costs (P&L): I calculate together with the related fixed asset or intangible asset (balance sheet)

    - Interest costs (P&L): I calculate together with the related loan(s) (balance sheet)

4. **Build in error checks where possible:** In the simple example above, the total costs in the P&L are calculated (cell F7) and as a check (cell F13) this figure is compared to the total costs in the calculations sheet. A non-zero result indicates there is an error, which you can then investigate and correct. The crucial topic of checks is covered in more detail in sub-chapter 5.1 'Build in error checks and a master check'.

3.8. BEST PRACTICE CHECKLIST

Get the basics right

- Decide if a spreadsheet is the right tool for the job

- Do not be complacent and think 'it will never happen to me'

- Get trained or use suitably trained staff

- Follow the Golden Ground Rules

- Always review and test your spreadsheets and ideally have someone else do that as well (so-called 'four eyes principle')

Mistakes in usage

- Organise your data well

  - Do not use hidden rows or hidden columns or otherwise hide data; use row/column groupings

  - If appropriate, group data into separate blocks

  - Consider extra column(s) for filtering

- Special tips for sensitive/confidential data

  - Be aware of the risks

  - Separate such data from the rest; if appropriate, store such data in a separate file with restricted access

  - Never send or publish Excel files with pivot tables based on sensitive/personal data; do not rely on pivot table options to protect this data

  - If you want to send or publish aggregated results (only), use PDFs or create a 'sent version' with only outputs and no data details; break all links to source files

- Use clear version control to ensure only the latest version of a spreadsheet file is used

  - Store spreadsheets on the server or in the cloud (OneDrive) and do not send via e-mail if you can avoid it

  - Use an agreed folder structure and an agreed model naming convention

  - If files are sent back and forth, be clear who has the 'master version'

Incorrect inputs

- Get the basics right

    - Know your business and train your users

    - Implement checks early in your spreadsheet development

    - Implement controls also in the surrounding processes e.g., expert review

- Organise your inputs and source documents

    - Obtain and store source documents

    - Clearly mark input data and quote your sources

- Avoid input errors

    - Follow the Golden Ground Rules, notably #4

    - Choose a suitable standard currency and unit for monetary values in your workbook and use it consistently throughout e.g., thousands of US Dollars

    - Only vary from the standard unit for good reason, and in such cases (i) clearly state the units used and (ii) always use the standard unit for results

    - Use clear labelling including units

    - Define and use a sign convention, e.g., income and cash inflows positive, costs and cash outflows negative, all balance sheet values generally positive

    - Construct your spreadsheet to reduce the risk of sign errors, e.g., inputs generally positive or use separate rows for positive and negative number inputs

    - Clearly mark any missing, uncertain or unknown inputs, for example, you can make the text red or the background yellow; review and update these before spreadsheet completion

- Use data validation

- Do not 'right align' cells with numbers or dates because this hide text numbers that you want to identify and correct

- Convert any numeric data stored as text to numbers: either multiply by one or use 'convert text to columns'

- Check for errors

  - Increase the visibility of significant inputs by showing them on the dashboard or cockpit

  - Use Excel background checks ('green corners')

  - Add checks on your totals

  - Check, validate and sense-check your inputs: ideally, get someone else to check them too

  - Review your results and if possible, compare to prior data: large, odd results or variances could indicate incorrect inputs

---

Hard-coded values

- Do not hard-code

- Always show data, assumptions, adjustments and factors clearly as inputs

- Clearly mark any temporary hard-coding used for test purposes and remove after testing

---

SUM and other calculation errors

- Use AutoSum, AutoAverage etc. to help you select the correct range but always check the range selected by Excel; in particular, watch out if you have gaps in your data

- For added rows (or columns) of data:

3. Learn from horror stories

- – Avoid adding new data above the first data row or below the last data row as these may well be excluded from the SUM

  – Use automatic range extension (Excel 2013 onwards) for rows added at the end

  – Alternatively, insert a blank line before the total and include this in the range for SUM, AVERAGE etc. so that row insertions at the end of the data are always included in the selected range

- Use an Excel table: new entries are automatically included in SUMs etc. and formulas are automatically copied to new rows

- Keep data and calculations together for clarity

  – Keep formulas next to the data used

  – Avoid cross-sheet calculations - use simple links only

- Avoid mathematical errors

  – Establish and use a sign convention consistently (already recommended)

  – Understand mathematical operator precedence: BODMAS = brackets, order (power of), division/multiplication, addition/subtraction

- Use the Warren Buffet rule of modelling: only model what you understand; if necessary, ask a subject-matter expert to assist you

- As always, test your model and review your results

- Interpretation: Even if your ranges and formulas are correct, always remember that correlation does not prove causality

---

Copy & paste and cut & paste errors

- General tips

  – Reduce the need for copy and paste actions e.g., by keeping everything you need in one file

- Reduce the need for cut and paste actions by using alternative functionality such as sorting, filtering and ranks or dynamic arrays, if available

- Do not use hidden rows or columns: these can be easily overlooked when copy & pasting, cut & pasting and analysing

- Copying data

  - Paste as values, not formulas

  - Ensure source and destination areas have the same structure and consider protecting sheets to prevent structural changes

  - Copy and paste the correct rows and columns: This is best achieved using range names

- Copying formulas

  - Test your calculations, especially if a section is to be copied; test it thoroughly to be as sure as you can that it is free of material error

  - Learn and correctly use $ cell-fixing (anchoring): as a general rule, fix as much as necessary but as little as possible

  - Check your data in sections copy-pasted from somewhere else: are inputs and assumptions valid for the new area?

Incorrect links

- Follow Golden Ground Rules #2 and #3 to ensure simplicity and consistency and so reduce the risk of in-sheet and cross-sheet link errors

- Add checks e.g., to test if totals on input and calculation sheets agree in actual periods, where there should be no difference

- Avoid or minimise links to external files

Circular errors and mistakes in logic

- General tips

  - Build in error checks where possible

  - Never do calculations in output sheets other than plus/minus, SUM and possibly simple KPIs

  - Calculate KPIs to act as sense-checkers

- Circular references

  - Design calculation logic in order to avoid circular references

  - Be aware of potential issues caused by using the iterations option or copy-paste macros

- Mixing up real and nominal figures or different currencies

  - Understand the terms real and nominal

  - As a general rule, always calculate and use nominal numbers (i.e., including inflation effects)

  - Agree on and clearly state the currency and units in use

- Double counting

  - Understand how double counting can occur

  - Calculate figures for the outputs in the same order as the outputs; if you break this rule, only do so for a valid reason and make it clear

4. Avoid common function errors

'Let me not pray to be sheltered from dangers,
but to be fearless in facing them.'
Rabindranath Tagore, the 'Bard of Bengal'

VLOOKUP is a much-loved function. I, too, was smitten once! But it has some traps for the unwary. Once I had discovered these and found better alternatives, I essentially stopped using it. Some other functions such as NPV (to calculate the net present value for a series of cash flows) and IRR (to calculate the internal rate of return for a series of cash flows), common in project and company valuations, as well as SUMIF(S) and IFERROR also have pitfalls. But forewarned is forearmed, so let us take a closer look so that you can avoid the dangers.

Here we focus on common potential errors and how to avoid them. It is all essential knowledge if you want to truly learn how to excel and create reliable spreadsheets.

4.1. VLOOKUP

Background: Which would have a bigger, negative impact: (i) a global recession or (ii) if VLOOKUP suddenly stopped working? Some assert that a VLOOKUP failure would lead to a bigger global meltdown. While this may be exaggerating the point, the fact is that VLOOKUP is widely used.

VLOOKUP means vertical look up. It has a sibling HLOOKUP for horizontal lookup but she does not get out much. The VLOOKUP function enables you to search for a specific value in one column of a block of data and get a value from another column. For example, you can look up a particular customer in a customer master data list and find out his credit limit or payment terms from another column in that list. This sort of functionality can be very useful and so the function is widely used in practice and has many fans. I used to use it a lot and was proud that I knew all of the function's arguments and how to use them. But sadly, it has a number of shortcomings and potential for errors. There are workarounds for some of these, but the good news is, there are better alternatives, which I recommend and explain below.

Error types and prevention:

1. **Non-unique lookup value:** You look up a month (e.g., month 1 = January) instead of the month and year combined (e.g., 20xx-01). VLOOKUP stops searching the moment it finds the first match, even if this is not what you wanted (e.g., wrong year), and gives you the result for that item. Or you look up customer name and the customer has several accounts for different cities and you get back the data for the Birmingham account when you wanted the London account.

    Prevent errors: Always ensure the value you are searching for exists in the source data only once. If necessary, you can combine data from multiple columns to create a unique reference: use the CONCATENATE function or simply join cell values together using '&' (the equivalent of '+' for text) e.g., Year cell & '-' & month cell. This can be rather cumbersome and the SUMIFS function does the job better because you can set multiple criteria using multiple columns in the source data.

2. **Lookup value is unique, but you searched for the nearest match (approximate match vs. exact match):** By default, VLOOKUP assumes the data is sorted in ascending order of the lookup column and returns the 'nearest match' (i.e., the last item that is not higher than the search value). This can be useful in some cases, e.g., when looking up a percentage discount based upon ranges: up to 20 units => 0% discount, 21 to 50 units => 5% discount and over 50 units => 10% discount. A VLOOKUP can get you the correct discount e.g., a customer has ordered 30 items, the discount is 5%. However, in 99%

of cases, you want it to find an exact match, so forgetting to set the relevant argument is a recipe for disaster.

Prevent errors: To find only an exact match is easy: at the end of the VLOOKUP function, you must enter FALSE (or 0 also works) for the [range_lookup] argument as shown below.

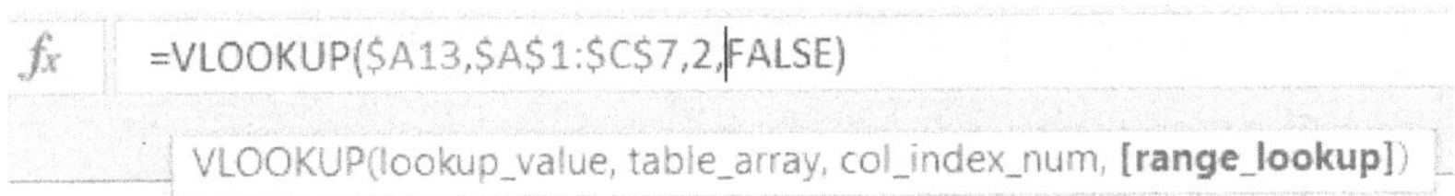

Although this solution is easy, it is also easy to forget this because [range_lookup] is an optional argument i.e., you do not have to enter it. We can see this because Excel has marked it in square brackets. If you omit it, Excel assumes you want an approximate match, which in my opinion is very unhelpful and leads to errors. It would have been better for Microsoft to have made this a required argument, or failing that, to assume that an exact match is wanted. And finally, the parameters FALSE and TRUE do not clearly represent what they mean, although to be fair, the Excel tool-tip which appears when you enter the function tells you.

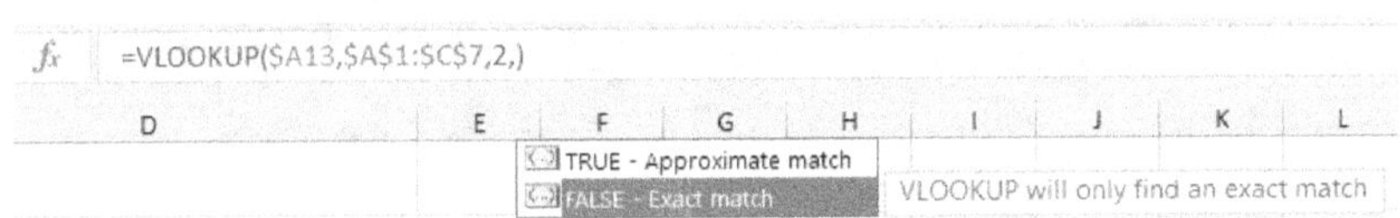

If you have Excel 365 you can use an improved lookup function called XLOOKUP which tackles many of the problems with VLOOKUP. It effectively combines INDEX and MATCH in a single function and adds in a few useful extra arguments, such as search order (first to last or last to first). It also assumes you want an exact match if you do not specify. Hurrah!

how2excel tip

Use the 'fx' icon to get function details

To get more information on this or any function, click on the 'fx' icon to the left of the formula (see screenshot above). You then get the function broken down into arguments (these are the values to be entered in brackets after the function's name) with a helpful description of the function's purpose and notes on each argument as the example screenshot for VLOOKUP below shows.

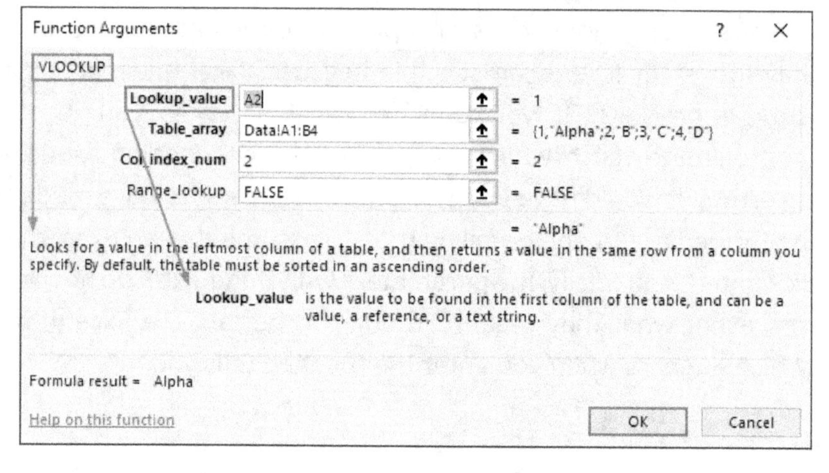

Click on the hyperlink 'Help on this function' in the lower left corner of the dialog window for additional details and examples. An alternative method to this help file is simply to select the relevant cell with the function and press F1. Nowadays, these help files often include useful videos.

3. **Lookup value does not exist in the source data:** Here you get an annoying #N/A error which feeds through to all dependent cells. This may be useful to know if you expect the source data to contain all the values that you are looking up, as it may help you to identify data errors. But quite often this is not the case.

Prevent errors: You could use the IFERROR function to return a zero or blank in the case of error. However, as I explain in sub-chapter 4.6, this is not best practice as it can hide errors that you would rather identify and correct. A better solution is to use SUMIF or SUMIFS... if the lookup value does not exist in the source data, you automatically get a zero. Alternatively, create a pivot table of the data; if set up correctly, this summarises the data automatically and can be easily amended to analyse the data in other ways.

Alternatively, for Office 365 users, use XLOOKUP, which has an optional argument where you can specify what result you want if no match is found.

4. **Lookup value is not in the first column of the source data:** In theory, you cannot use VLOOKUP. But users are ingenious, and I have seen them copy (or move) the relevant data column to the left of the data so that it is in the first column. This changes the source data, however, which is generally not best practice (the 'look but don't touch' principle) as it can create other errors and is more difficult to update with new or revised data.

   Prevent errors: A better solution is XLOOKUP (if you have Office 365), INDEX and MATCH combined (see below) or possibly SUMIFS.

5. **A column gets inserted in (or deleted from) the source data:** This is a common error. The problem with VLOOKUP is that you have to specify the column number of the data you want. If someone inserts, deletes, or moves one or more columns between the lookup value column and the column with the data you want, Excel does not amend the formula for you, and you get the wrong answer. This is also a problem if you copy a VLOOKUP formula to the right, expecting it to get the data from subsequent columns in the source data – think again! In both cases, the column number is not updated by Excel because it is simply a number.

   Prevent errors: One workaround here is to use the function COLUMN to give you the column number you need for the

VLOOKUP formula instead of just typing the column number, but this can get complicated if the lookup value is not in column A of the data to be searched. As noted above, a better solution is XLOOKUP (if you have Office 365), INDEX and MATCH combined (see below) or possibly SUMIFS. For all these functions, Excel uses column letters for the links which are automatically updated if columns are inserted, deleted or moved.

6. **The lookup value occurs more than once in the source data:** Maybe you want the sum e.g., of all sales to customer XYZ, not just the first sale value. VLOOKUP can only ever give you the first value, so it is the wrong function to use.

   Prevent errors: Use SUMIFS. Here there is also some potential for error, but this is easily avoided as you will see below when I cover this very useful function in more detail.

7. **VLOOKUP creates too many unnecessary linkages which makes testing difficult:** This is not an error but nevertheless a further disadvantage when using VLOOKUP. When you are analysing your model using auditing tools (see chapter 6 'Find and correct errors'), you often want to trace precedents or dependents of a particular cell. Let us use the following example to illustrate the problems associated with a formula using VLOOKUP.

f_x | =VLOOKUP(A2,'Customer master data'!$D:$Z,18,FALSE)

   This formula takes the customer name in cell A2 of the current sheet and looks for it in the sheet 'Customer master data' in column D and returns the value in column 18 (numbering from column D = column 1), which should be the agreed payment terms in days. VLOOKUP causes two problems:

i) VLOOKUP formulas have too many precedents: When tracing precedents of this VLOOKUP formula, you will find the whole source data table (Customer master data sheet, columns D to Z) is identified and it is not always easy to identify the lookup column giving the result unless the data table used is small. In the above example, can you quickly identify which is column 18 starting from column D? You cannot simply assume it is the last column referenced: in the above case this is column Z, which would be wrong (the correct answer is column U). Finding the correct column is like playing 'Where's Wally?' but without the fun – it is tiresome and time-wasting, not to mention error-prone.

ii) VLOOKUP source data tables have too many dependents: It is a similar story when trying to trace dependents from source data. All columns referenced in any VLOOKUP formula (in the above example, columns D to Z) are shown as having dependents, when in reality only two are used by the VLOOKUP formula: the looked-up column D with the customer name and the column with the payment terms data that is being retrieved, column U.

These two features represent red herrings for model detective work and so also here, VLOOKUP gets a big thumbs down from me.

Prevent errors: The alternatives XLOOKUP, INDEX and MATCH, and SUMIF(S) do not suffer from these disadvantages – with these functions you can always clearly identify the precedent and dependent cells or ranges and there are no extraneous columns in sight. A big thumbs up!

Summary of recommendations:

---

1. **Do not use VLOOKUP or HLOOKUP** since there is too much potential for error and they also suffer from other disadvantages, such as confusing audit trails when testing models. Use better alternatives instead.

2. **Use XLOOKUP** if you have Office 365. This avoids many of the issues with VLOOKUP and effectively combines the flexibility of IFERROR, INDEX and MATCH... wow!

3. **Use INDEX and MATCH or SUMIFS** if you have an older version of Excel, since these functions have significantly less potential for error and do not suffer from audit trail problems (which I explain in more detail below).

4.2. INDEX AND MATCH

If you have Office 365 you can use XLOOKUP. But not all users do, so INDEX and MATCH is generally my preferred solution as it works in all Excel versions. Here is an example so you can see how it works and better understand the advantages.

	A	B	C	D	E
		Sales 20xx	Sales		
1	Branch	(TEUR)	area (m²)	[Cell] Formula	
2	Berlin	200	120	(inputs)	
3	Düsseldorf	240	100	(inputs)	
4	Frankfurt	180	80	(inputs)	
5	Hamburg	150	90	(inputs)	
6	München	400	220	(inputs)	
7	Stuttgart	300	150	(inputs)	
8	Totals	1,470	760	[B8] =SUM(B2:B7)	
9					
10	INDEX and MATCH in one step				
		Sales 20xx	Sales		
11		(TEUR)	area (m²)		
12	Düsseldorf	240	100	[B12] =INDEX(B$2:B$7, MATCH($A12,$A$2:$A$7,0))	
13					
14	INDEX and MATCH in two steps				
			Sales 20xx	Sales	
15		Match	(TEUR)	area (m²)	
16	Düsseldorf	2	240	100	[B16] =MATCH($A16,$A$2:$A$7,0)
17					[C16] =INDEX(B$2:B$7,$B16)

The example shown above is for a German retail company with six branches in big cities. We have a list of the branches, plus input cells containing their sales for the year, plus the size of their sales area in square metres. Below that (in reality, probably on a different sheet) we want to input a branch name of our choice and get back the sales value and floor space for that branch.

INDEX returns the Nth value from a specified column; the position N is determined using the MATCH function which finds the position of the unique 'lookup' value in a specified column. Similar to VLOOKUP, MATCH also has an optional argument at the end to determine if you are seeking an exact match (enter 0; as a rule, this is what you want) or an approximate match (enter 1 or -1; press F1 for help on these options).

The INDEX and MATCH function columns are specified using column letters and so are automatically updated by Excel if columns change. Just what you need to avoid errors. And as I already mentioned, when testing your spreadsheet, precedents and dependents are correctly identified by formula auditing tools (more on those in chapter 6 'Find and correct errors').

Although this solution requires two functions, I find it is not more complicated than VLOOKUP and it also does not suffer from the many disadvantages associated with VLOOKUP, noted above. You can also split the two functions into two steps to make the calculation easier to understand (see second example above). This is to be recommended if you are retrieving multiple items of data, say various fields from a list of customer master data. For a given customer, each field you retrieve will be in the same row of the source data, so why calculate the MATCH value every time? Calculate it once and refer to this cell for each INDEX function (the COUNT principle = Calculate Once, Use Numerous Times). This can save you valuable Excel calculation time, which can be very useful for large data analysis spreadsheets.

Error types and prevention:

Mismatched ranges: In the example above, cell B12, the INDEX range covers rows 2 to 7 (B$2:B$7), so the MATCH range must also cover rows 2 to 7 (A$2:A$7). Failing to match these will cause errors.

Prevent errors: Quite easy really – just double-check that the rows (or possibly columns) in your INDEX and MATCH ranges agree. A good way to help do this can be to format your source data a table (Ctrl T). Alternatively, you can define your ranges to be entire columns (e.g., B:B instead of B$2:B$7) but this can slow down calculations. Whatever your approach, always check a few results produced by your INDEX-MATCH formula by manually searching for the correct answer.

4.3. SUMIF AND SUMIFS

Background: These two functions are very useful. They allow you to sum up items from a given column of data if the values in one or more other columns match certain criteria that you define. So, for example, you can sum all sales to customer BigCo (one condition: customer name). Or all sales of widgets to customer BigCo in January of this year (three conditions: product, customer name and month of sale). If you only have one condition, you can use SUMIF or SUMIFS, if you have more than one, you must use SUMIFS.

Error types and prevention:

1.   Adding conditions to a SUMIF formula

If you have just one condition, it seems natural to use SUMIF rather than SUMIFS. But if you later have to add a second condition, you must switch to SUMIFS. That can be a challenge because with SUMIFS, the order of the arguments is different to SUMIF as shown below.

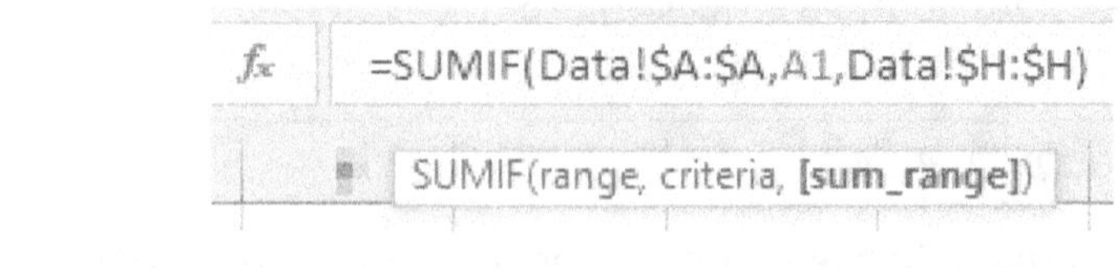

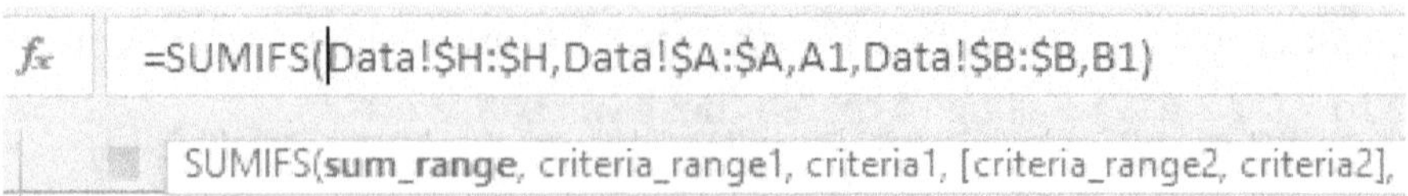

In SUMIF the sum range is the last argument, in SUMIFS it is the first argument. When writing or amending a formula, there is a risk that you mix up the sum range and criteria range.

Prevent errors:

I recommend that you generally use the function SUMIFS, even if you only have one condition. Then there can be no confusion about the order of arguments: first the sum range, then the condition(s) and you can easily add more conditions later, if necessary.

Only use the function SUMIF if the sum range is the same as the criteria range e.g., sum all sales over 10,000. (That is why the sum_range argument for SUMIF is optional i.e., shown in square brackets in the tool-tip).

2. Mismatched ranges

Similar to INDEX and MATCH, it is possible to mismatch the sum range and criteria range(s) such that e.g., the sum range covers rows 5 to 100, the criteria range covers rows 6 to 101. Thus, if the criteria in row 6 is met, the value in row 5 (not row 6) will be added.

Prevent errors: Again, quite easy really – just double-check that the rows (or possibly columns) in your sum range and criteria range(s) agree. Alternatively (as in the example shown above), you can define your ranges to be entire columns (e.g., H:H instead of H$5:H$100) but this can slow down calculations. Additionally, always check a few results produced by your SUMIFS formula by manually filtering and adding the source data.

4.4. NPV (Net Present Value)

Background: NPV is a great function commonly used in assessing projects and in valuing companies using cash flows and the concept of the time-value of money. This is the principle that £100 today is worth more than £100 in a year's time, and even more than £100 in five years' time due to the effects of inflation; and also due to the fact that you could invest £100 today and it would grow to a larger value in the future.

Imagine there is a project where you could invest £1 million today and get back £1.1 million in one year, is this worth investing in? It all depends on your cost of capital. If you know this (for example, you expect a 6% p.a. return on projects of a similar risk), you can use the NPV function to answer this question. It takes the expected cash flows from the project and works out how much these add up to in 'today's money'. This process is called discounting and the result is the net present value, which tells you the sum of all the cash flows, both negative and positive, expressed in today's money (the present values). Here are the decision-making rules:

- If you end up with a positive NPV, this means you would earn more than your expected rate of return (if all goes according to plan) and so the project is, in theory, worth investing in.

- If the NPV is nil, it does not mean that you earn nothing. It means that you would earn your expected rate of return (assuming things turn out as planned). You would be undecided about such a project – you could have earned the same return by investing in another project of similar size and risk. Bear in mind, however, that if things turn out worse than planned (and projects often have cost overruns), you will end up with a negative NPV in practice. Which brings us to negative NPVs.

- If the NPV is negative, then it is not worth investing in the project – theoretically, you could have earned more by investing your money in another project of similar size and risk.

- If you have two projects with positive NPVs and you have enough money and resources for both, then in theory you should do both of them, as both should give you a return above your expectations. If they are mutually exclusive i.e., you can only invest in one or the other, then you should choose the project with the biggest, positive NPV.

The example £1 million project mentioned above has an NPV of around £38,000. According to the above rules, it would be worth investing in this project.

NPV is a great concept and a practical Excel function but there are a couple of things to watch out for that are best illustrated with some examples. In the following section, I compare and contrast these examples with results using the IRR function.

Error types and prevention:

	A	B	C	D	E	F	G	H
1	WACC (Cost of Capital)	6.0%						
2								
3	All values are in TEUR (thousands of Euros)							
4								
5	NPV and free cash flows	NPV	Year 1	Year 2	Year 3	Year 4	Year 5	[Cell] Formula
6	Case 1	93	(1,000)	100	350	400	450	[B6] =NPV(B$1;C6:G6)
7	Case 2	4	(1,000)	0	350	400	450	[B7] =NPV(B$1;C7:G7)
8	Case 3 (incorrect)	60	(1,000)		350	400	450	[B8] =NPV(B$1;C8:G8)
9	Case 4 (equivalent)	60	(1,000)	350	400	450		[B9] =NPV(B$1;C9:G9)
10	Case 5	93	94	(1,060)	350	400	450	[B10] =NPV(B$1;C10:G10)
11	Case 6	926	(10,000)	1,000	3,500	4,000	4,500	[B11] =NPV(B$1;C11:G11)
12								
13	NPV and free cash flows		Year 0	Year 1	Year 2	Year 3	Year 4	[Cell] Formula
14	Case 7 (incorrect)	93	(1,000)	100	350	400	450	[B14] =NPV(B$1;C14:G14)
15	Case 8 (correct)	98	(1,000)	100	350	400	450	[B15] =C15+NPV(B$1;D15:G15)
16								
17	Case 8 "manual method"							
18	Discount factor		1.0000	0.9434	0.8900	0.8396	0.7921	[D18] =C18/(1+$B$1)
19	NPV and PV of cashflows	98	(1,000)	94	311	336	356	[B19] =SUM(C19:G19)
20								[C19] =C15*C18

The screenshot above shows a number of cases to illustrate various points, all using a WACC (weighted average cost of capital) of 6.0%, which is clearly labelled and shown as a (grey) input cell in cell B1. This complies with Golden Ground Rule #3 – put simply, consistency, including clear marking of input cells.

Case 1: Typical project cash flows i.e., a big outflow to start and then a number of cash inflows. This example produces a positive NPV of 93 TEUR, so the project earns more than the cost of capital.

Case 2: Here we have changed the 100 TEUR cash flow in year 2 to zero. As expected, the NPV drops (we have less cash inflows) and the NPV is now just 4 TEUR.

4. Avoid common function errors

Potential error: blank cell

Case 3 (error): Here we have deleted the cash flow in year 2 i.e., the cell is blank. It looks the same as case 2, so I would expect to get the same answer, but we get a higher figure of 60 TEUR. This is an error. To see what Excel has done, let us look at case 4.

Case 4: Here we have the same cash flows as in row 6 but I have closed the gap by moving the cash flows in years 3 to 5 into years 2 to 4. This gives the same NPV result as in case 3 and shows what Excel has done there – it has ignored the blank cell and taken the following figures (from years 3 to 5) and assumed they occur in years 2 to 4. That is not what I expected or wanted in case 3.

Prevent errors: to avoid the type of error in case 3, never have blanks in your cash flows and use zeros instead.

Case 5: Here I have taken the cash flows from case 1 and swapped the cash flows in years 1 and 2. To be comparable with case 1, I multiplied the year 1 cash flow by 1.06 to get a year 2 equivalent value (with a WACC of 6%) and divided the year 2 cash flow by 1.06 to get a year 1 equivalent value. The NPV result of 93 TEUR is the same as in case 1. That makes sense. I include this example in order to contrast it with the IRR calculation of the same cash flows in the next set of examples below.

Case 6: Here I have taken the cash flows from case 1 and multiplied them all by ten. The resulting NPV is 926 TEUR or ten times the NPV of case 1. That makes sense. I also include this example in order to contrast it with the IRR calculation of the same cash flows in the next set of examples below.

Cases 1 to 6 all have the first cash flow occurring in year 1. It is important to know that the NPV function assumes that the first cash flow occurs one period (in this case one year) in the future and so will discount all cash flows including the first one. Often, however, the first cash flow is when the project starts, and this is the point in time when you want the NPV, so let us look at an example of that.

Potential error: Cash flow at the start of a project

Case 7 (error): Here I have taken the cash flows from case 1 but now they start in year 0 (start of project) and end in year 4. Using the NPV function gives the same answer as in case 1, which is clearly wrong – all cash flows are happening a year earlier than in case 1, so the NPV must be larger.

Prevent errors:

Case 8: Shows the correct way to calculate the NPV in such cases: the cash flow in year 0 should not be discounted so take that and then add the NPV of the subsequent cash flows.

Case 8 'manual method': I have also calculated the NPV 'the long way' using discount factors instead of the NPV function to calculate the present value of each year's cash flow. Adding these up gives the NPV, which in this case is 98 TEUR, the same answer as in case 8 with the NPV function, so I am confident it is correct. This is always a good way of testing an NPV result, to detect and, if necessary, correct any errors. In fact, it is a good check principle: calculate a number two different ways and compare the results, which should be the same. We cover this principle in more detail in sub-chapter 5.1 'Build in error checks and a master check'.

Potential error: non-annual periods

In all the above examples we have used periods of years. In such cases, the WACC must also be for a year (per annum).

Prevent errors: If you have (say) monthly periods, then the WACC must be the value for a month, not a year, otherwise you will get incorrect results.

Potential error: unequal periods

What if cash flows are occurring after periods of unequal length? If you have periods of unequal length in your model then you are breaking a key part of Golden Ground Rule #3: Consistency is key. Having said that, it can be justifiable for projects to have a period structure of (say) the first two years monthly and the following five years annually. This is because (i) the timing and value of cash flows at the start of the project are typically known with more accuracy than later cash flows and (ii) the discounting effect changes more significantly in the early years than in the later years, and the effect on the NPV can be material.

Prevent errors: Simply use periods of equal length. If you insist on using periods of unequal length, however, then follow the following rules to reduce the risk of error.

1. You must use the function XNPV (extended NPV) instead of NPV, which requires not just the cash flows but also the related dates to be referred to in the function. Alternatively, use the 'manual method' from case 8 above.

2. Use clearly labelled and consistent time period blocks. In the above example, that would be (block 1) two years of monthly periods (24 periods) followed by (block 2) five years of annual periods (five periods).

3. Take great care with your cash flow formulas and discount factors (if relevant) in both period blocks to ensure they take account of the different period lengths.

4. I also recommend having a blank column between the two period blocks to visually separate them and also to reduce the risk that you copy a 'monthly formula' into a column requiring an 'annual formula' or vice versa.

Summary of recommendations:

1. **Mind the gap!** Ensure there are no gaps in your cash flows.

2. **Take care if the first cash flow is at year 0 (often called t_0 or time 0):** this cash flow should not be discounted, so take this into account in your formula and do not simply 'NPV' all cash flows.

3. **Check your NPV result mathematically:** Try calculating the result twice, once with the NPV function and again 'manually' using discount factors in each period.

4. **Remember the answer is merely indicative:** Actual cash flows will differ to plan cash flows, and this will affect the NPV. This is particularly important to bear in mind if you are using the NPV to help you make an important decision, such as the purchase price for a company acquisition.

5. **Calculate a range of values:** Typically, calculate NPVs for base, best- and worst-case scenarios. Or use Monte Carlo simulation to generate 1000s of scenarios. These should help you assess the range of possible values, and you can also take action to improve the chances of the best case and/or reduce the chances of the worst case occurring.

6. **Carry out a sense-check:** Calculate an implied multiple or perform a multiple valuation as a sense-check on your NPV result.

These last two points are outside the scope of this book, but there is plenty of literature on company valuations as well as useful websites.

4.5. IRR (Internal Rate of Return)

Background: IRR is another function commonly used in assessing project cash flows. It is expressed as a percentage and tells you the discount rate at which the cash flows give you an NPV of nil, in other words, it represents the rate of return on the project (hence the name).

Imagine we are assessing the same project we mentioned before when we looked at NPV: you could invest £1 million today and expect to get back £1.1 million in one year, is this project worth investing in? It all depends on your cost of capital. If you know this (for example, you expect a 6% return on projects of a similar risk), you can also use the IRR function to answer this question.

Here are the decision-making rules, according to theory:

- If the IRR is greater than your cost of capital, then you would earn more than your expected rate of return (if all goes according to plan) and so the project is, in theory, worth investing in.

- If the IRR equals your cost of capital, you would earn your required rate of return if things turn out as planned. Bear in mind, however, that if things turn out worse than planned, you will end up with an IRR lower than your cost of capital in practice.

- If the IRR is less than your cost of capital, then it is not worth investing in the project – you want to earn a bigger return on a project of this risk.

- If you have two projects with IRRs above your cost of capital and you have enough money and resources for both, then in theory you should do both of them, as both should give you a return above your expectations. If they are mutually exclusive i.e., you can only invest in one or the other, then you should choose the project with the biggest IRR which is larger than your cost of capital.

- Your cost of capital is sometimes called the hurdle rate, which the IRR must exceed. Some companies add (say) 2% to their cost of capital to determine the hurdle rate. They do this to take uncertainties in the cash flows into account and 'to be on the safe side'. But it is perhaps better to perform sensitivity analysis to assess the potential impact of such risks.

The 1-million-pound project mentioned above has an IRR of 10%, which is higher than the stated cost of capital of 6%. According to the IRR rules noted above, it would be worth investing in this project. In this example, the result is consistent with the NPV answer above, but this is not always the case, which is an important point you need to understand and which I address below.

IRR is a valuable concept and another useful Excel function but there are a couple of other things to watch out for that are best illustrated with some examples. In the following section, I use the same cases as in the NPV function above to better compare and contrast them. In these cases, there is no cost of capital (WACC) needed for the calculations – your WACC simply serves as the hurdle rate which IRR has to exceed for a project to be financially worthwhile.

Error types and prevention:

	A	B	C	D	E	F	G	H
1	All values are in TEUR (thousands of Euros)							
2								
3	IRR and free cash flows	IRR	Year 1	Year 2	Year 3	Year 4	Year 5	[Cell] Formula
4	Case 1	9.5%	(1,000)	100	350	400	450	[B4] =IRR(C4:G4)
5	Case 2	6.1%	(1,000)	0	350	400	450	[B5] =IRR(C5:G5)
6	Case 3 (incorrect)	9.3%	(1,000)		350	400	450	[B6] =IRR(C6:G6)
7	Case 4 (equivalent)	9.3%	(1,000)	350	400	450		[B7] =IRR(C7:G7)
8	Case 5 (misleading)	11.8%	94	(1,060)	350	400	450	[B8] =IRR(C8:G8)
9	Case 6	9.5%	(10,000)	1,000	3,500	4,000	4,500	[B9] =IRR(C9:G9)
10								
11	IRR and free cash flows		Year 0	Year 1	Year 2	Year 3	Year 4	[Cell] Formula
12	Case 7	9.5%	(1,000)	100	350	400	450	[B12] =IRR(C12:G12)
13								
14	Case 7 "manual method"							
15	Discount factor		1.0000	0.9130	0.8335	0.7609	0.6947	[D15] =C15/(1+$B$12)
16	NPV and PV of cashflows	-	(1,000)	91	292	304	313	[D16] =D12*D15

The screenshot above shows the same cash flow examples we saw in the NPV discussions above, to facilitate a comparison of the two methods.

Case 1: Typical project cash flows i.e., a big outflow to start and then several cash inflows. This example produces a positive IRR of 9.5%, above the WACC of 6.0%. This seems plausible as we had a positive NPV from the same cash flows.

Case 2: With nil in year 2, the IRR reduces (as we would expect) to 6.1%. This is just above the WACC of 6% and so is still worth investing in, according to the rules. This seems plausible as we had a small positive NPV from the same cash flows.

Potential error: blank cell

Case 3 (incorrect): When the year 2 cash flow is deleted, Excel calculates a different IRR to Case 2, which is incorrect. (The NPV was also incorrect in this case).

Case 4: This shows how Excel has calculated case 3 – as in the same case with NPV, it has ignored the blank cell and taken the following figures (from years 3 to 5) and assumed they occur in years 2 to 4. That is not what I expected or wanted.

Prevent errors: We come to the same conclusion we arrived at with NPVs: to avoid errors of this type never have blanks in your cash flows. Use zeros if appropriate.

Potential decision error: multiple changes in cash flow direction

Case 5: Again, we have the same cash flows as in the corresponding NPV case above. The NPV gave the same result as in case 1 because the two cases are mathematically equivalent. But with IRR we get a different result: the IRR in case 1 was 9.5%, in case 5 we have 11.8%. If you make your decision based purely upon IRR, you would pick case 5 over case 1 even though they are mathematically equivalent, as the NPV results demonstrate. This shows a weakness of IRR, which can arise when there is more than one change of sign in the cash flows (from negative to positive cash flows or vice versa). There can even be more than one IRR for a series of cash flows that produce an NPV of nil, typically when there are multiple changes of sign in the cash flows – the IRR function gives you just one of them.

Prevent errors: Do not use IRR on its own, only in addition to other results, typically NPV.

Potential decision error: projects of different size

Case 6: Here the cash flows are 10 times those in case 1 but we get the same IRR. If you make your decision based purely upon IRR, you could pick case 1 or case 6, they have the same IRR. However, the NPV results clearly demonstrate: case 6 gives you ten times more money as case 1, which is logical as the cash flows are ten times bigger.

Prevent errors: Once again, do not use IRR on its own, only in addition to other results, typically NPV.

Case 7: For IRR, it is irrelevant if the first cash flow is in year 0 or year 1, the IRR is the same, so we have no error and no case 8 here. To prove this, I have calculated the NPV in case 7 using the 'manual method' and discount factors taking account of the fact the first period is time 0 (discount factor 1) and thereafter using a discount rate equal to the calculated IRR of 9.5%. This calculation gives an NPV of zero, which proves the IRR result – by definition, the IRR is the discount rate which gives an NPV of zero.

Potential decision error: reinvestment rate

An additional limitation of IRR is that it assumes excess cash flows can be invested at the IRR rate. If the IRR is much higher than effective interest income rates (especially true in times of low interest rates) then this can also lead to a misleading result.

Prevent errors: In such cases it is better to use the function MIRR (modified IRR) – here you need to define both the finance rate and the reinvest rate in addition to the cash flows. See Excel help for more details if you want to use that. And as with IRR, do not use MIRR on its own.

Potential error: unequal periods

Like NPV, if your periods are not of equal length you will get an error using IRR.

Prevent errors: Use the function XIRR (extended IRR) and define the dates in addition to the cash flows.

Summary of recommendations:

1. **Be aware of the limitations of IRR:** It takes no account of size, the recommendation can disagree with NPV, it assumes that excess cash is invested at the IRR rate, there can be multiple solutions, unequal periods are a problem. Wow, that is a lot of limitations! You can get round some of these by using XIRR or MIRR, but really the best thing to do is to follow my second recommendation...

2. **Do not use IRR on its own**: Only use it in addition to other results, typically NPV or XNPV for unequal periods.

4.6. IFERROR

Background: At first sight, IFERROR seems to be a useful function: it allows you to avoid getting an error result if, for example, you divide by zero or if a looked-up value does not exist. But here I feel we are rejecting an error-detection gift from Excel: if there is an error, you really want to know about it so you can fix it.

Error types and prevention:
A 'true error' remains undetected

If you use IFERROR in combination with (for example) a VLOOKUP or INDEX and MATCH formula, expecting to find all items, then you will not notice if an item was not found, because the #N/A result is effectively suppressed.

Prevent errors: Avoid using IFERROR if you can, use with caution if you can't. Instead, amend your formulas to test only for specific causes such as zero as divisor.

In some cases, you need to validly exclude e.g., a division by zero if you are calculating the percentage rise in sales from the prior period and in one case the prior period happens to have zero sales. In cases like this, I recommend that you test if the denominator is zero and only exclude this problem, like this:

= IF (sales last period cell = 0, "n/a", sales this period / sales last period - 1)

Notice I use "n/a" (or "" blank cell) for a case where no value can be calculated, not zero. Zero % is the correct answer only when the sales in both periods are the same. This approach means that only division by zero errors (which can occur) are excluded, all other potential errors (such as #REF, #VALUE) are not excluded and you can therefore easily identify them if they occur (thanks, Excel!) and fix them.

4.7. BEST PRACTICE CHECKLIST

- VLOOKUP and HLOOKUP: Avoid these functions and use XLOOKUP, INDEX and MATCH, or SUMIFS instead

- INDEX and MATCH: Ensure INDEX and MATCH ranges use the same rows (or columns)

- SUMIF/SUMIFS:

  - As a rule, use SUMIFS in preference to SUMIF, to avoid a change in the order of arguments if you add more criteria

  - Ensure sum range and criteria range use the same rows (or columns)

- NPV: Ensure there are no gaps in your cash flows; do not discount cash flows at time zero

- IRR: Be aware of the limitations of IRR, most notably that it takes no account of size; use modified versions XIRR and MIRR if appropriate and do not use IRR on its own, only in addition to other results, typically NPV

- IFERROR: Avoid using IFERROR if you can, use with caution if you can't. It can hide errors that you should know about and correct; instead, test for the potential error e.g., the divisor is zero

5. Detect errors

'Houston, we have a problem.'
John ('Jack') Swigert, Apollo 13 astronaut (impactful misquote)

Hopefully, you have prepared well (chapter 1), followed Gary's Golden Ground Rules (chapter 2) and learnt from horror stories (chapter 3) and so your spreadsheet is free of errors! Or is it? A favourite saying of mine from Germany is 'trust is good, but control is better'. So how do you control your spreadsheet?

As in the Apollo 13 mission, it is essential that you first try to detect any problems that may arise, in case prevention fails (this chapter). And then you need to find and correct them (next chapter). I have split these two topics for clarity. In reality, however, there is often no clear division between the two. For example, if you find an incorrect formula, you have at once both detected and found the cause of the error. In other cases, however, such as when the balance sheet does not balance (error detected), you will need to adopt a systematic approach to find the cause and then correct the error, which we cover in the next chapter 'Find and correct errors'. But first, let us see how we can detect them. And rest assured, there are always some to detect. To do that, you just need to follow my three-pronged approach to error detection:

(1) Build checks into your spreadsheet

(2) Review and test your spreadsheet

(3) Get an independent review and test

Let us take a look at each of these steps in turn.

5.1. BUILD IN ERROR CHECKS AND A MASTER CHECK

Error checks are essential in all but the simplest spreadsheets. They cannot identify all errors but they do increase reliability. Sadly, we cannot say that a spreadsheet where no check errors have been identified has no errors. But we can say with some confidence that if there is a check error then there is a least one error in the spreadsheet. Please add error checks liberally throughout your workbook, wherever possible. They can check

- Accuracy – is a value correct?

- Completeness – are all items shown?

- Validity – is the value allowed?

I prefer to write my check formulas such that a result of zero means that no error has been identified e.g., = total assets - total liabilities. If both values are equal, as they should be, the check result is zero and no error is identified by the check. If it is non-zero, you get an idea of the size of the error.

Checks are typically one of the following five types.

1. Two different values agree (accuracy check)

The most important check for financial models consists of testing whether the balance sheet balances, i.e., total assets = total equity and liabilities in every model period and for every entity (e.g., group company) depicted in the model. (If you use the 'net assets' representation, the sum of net assets must equal the sum of equity, but the principle is the same). This will help you to identify potentially significant errors in your model.

In project financing models, it is good practice to include a 'sources and uses of funds' statement. Here, the total sources of funds (money in) must equal the total uses of funds (money out) for a given period, e.g., the build phase or the whole project lifecycle.

2. Two different calculations of the same value agree (accuracy check)

	A	B	C	D	E	F	G	H
1	TEUR	Data - Sales inputs or calculations				Outputs - Sales waterfall		[Cell] Formula
2								
3	Brand	20x1	20x2	Change		Sales in 20x1	420	[G3] =B8
4	A	120	160	+40		Brand A change	+40	[G4] =D4
5	B	80	100	+20		Brand B change	+20	[G5] =D5
6	C	220	150	-70		Brand C change	-70	[G6] =D6
7	D	-	140	+140		Sales in 20x2	410	[G7] =SUM(G3:G6)
8	Total	420	550	+130		Check	(140)	[G8] =G7-C8

The example above shows on the left-hand side a breakdown of sales by brand for two years plus the change in each case. On the right-hand side, we see a so-called waterfall table showing how the sales in the first year have been affected by the changes in sales of each brand. The total year 1 sales plus/minus all the changes by brand should equal the total sales in year two. A check identifies that there is a difference of 140 TEUR and so we have detected an error. In this simple case, the cause is obvious: the new brand D is missing from the waterfall calculation but in more complex examples, such a check can be very useful to identify errors that would perhaps would have gone unnoticed and uncorrected.

Notes on presentation

Notice that the change cells in columns D and G are formatted to show a clear + or - in front of the values, as appropriate, using custom formatting. To do this, select relevant cells, then press Ctrl 1 (cell format). Select the tab "Number" and the category "Custom". In the "Type" field enter this formatting code +#.##0_(;-#.##0_(;-_(and press OK.

It is useful to depict the waterfall values (shown in column G above) in a waterfall chart. This is only available as a standard graph type in Excel from Office 2016, but you can create your own – see the above-mentioned file.

3. The totals of certain figures flowing through the model agree (accuracy check)

Check that totals of certain figures – such as costs on output, calculation and input sheets – agree, where relevant. See the end of sub-chapter 3.7 'Circular errors and mistakes in logic' (section on 'double counting') for an example where total costs in the P&L are compared to total costs on the calculation sheet.

I use this one in financial models to check that the total profit in the financial statements (outputs) equals the total profit in the inputs in all 'actual' periods. This is a great check as it covers all manner of possible errors in transferring P&L data through the model.

4. There are no missing items (completeness check)

Check if any items on one sheet are missing from another. For example, on one sheet you have a system report of **actual** sales by product. On a second sheet, you **plan** the sales by product. This sheet should include all the products which you have actually sold, plus it may include new products. To help ensure that the **plan sheet** has a complete list of products, you can add checks to identify if any products on the **actual sheet** are missing and add them.

Here it always important to place the check on the sheet with the complete list to see if all items can be found on the other sheet. In a blank column, use the invaluable MATCH function (with the optional match-type = 0, meaning exact match) to see if the item e.g., a product code exists on the other sheet. If the list is long, you can use the function COUNTIFS, to count the number of match formulas with a result of #N/A. If the count is zero, then no missing items were identified. If non-zero, filter the list to show the #N/A results – which represent the missing items – and add these to the sheet where they are missing.

As shown in the above screenshot examples, always try to put such check formulas on the relevant worksheet next to the numbers they are checking. This proximity concept is general best practice, not just for checks. When performing checks or other calculations, you should have all the data you need just before (or at least near to) the calculation. This makes it easier to write and understand the formula and so reduces the risk of error. It also makes it easier to review when you are testing and searching for errors. Finally, link the check results to the master check sheet (see below).

5. Values are in expected ranges (validity check)

Check if a calculated value lies outside an allowed or expected range e.g., is positive but should be negative or is non-zero.

	A	B	C	D	E	F	G	H	I	J	K	L
1		Sales planning										[Cell] Formula
2												
3		Sales			Units			Average sales price				
4	Product	20x1	20x2		20x1	20x2		20x1	20x2	Change	Check	
5		TEUR	TEUR		units	units		EUR	EUR	%	10.0%	limit
7	X	1,200	1,728		120	160		10.00	10.80	8.0%	OK	[K7] =IF(ABS(J7)>=K$5,"Over limit","OK")
8	Y	2,240	2,550		280	30		8.00	85.00	962.5%	Over limit	[K8] =IF(ABS(J8)>=K$5,"Over limit","OK")
9	Z	3,840	3,080		320	280		12.00	11.00	-8.3%	OK	[K9] =IF(ABS(J9)>=K$5,"Over limit","OK")
10	Total	7,280	7,358		720	470		10.11	15.66	54.8%		
11									Check count		1	[K11] =COUNTIF(K7:K9,"<>OK")

In the above example, the average sales prices by product have been calculated as well as the percentage change. In the final column, there is a test to see if the change is more than the input limit of 10%. (An input here is best practice: no hard-coding in the check formulas!) A potential error ('over limit') has been identified for product Y. Upon investigation, the spreadsheet user finds they have input the units in year 2 incorrectly, the figure should have been 300 units. After correction, all checks are OK.

In each case, you need to calculate a check result, ideally to give a zero result when no error is identified. Is it acceptable to round check results?

Rounding of check results

Sometimes a small, non-zero check result is simply rounding. This can occur because your computer performs its calculations in binary (base 2) but the inputs and outputs you see are in decimal (base 10).

Conversions between the two can create tiny rounding differences which then emerge as 'check errors', which they are not really. To avoid this, simply round the check formula to (say) the nearest unit, by which I mean the nearest (say) whole dollar, even if the 'reporting currency' in your workbook is millions of dollars. In this example, you would round to 6 decimal places. Otherwise, you could find errors being 'rounded away'.

Checks on percentage figures are best multiplied by 100 otherwise a check such as '= 100% - (cell with percentage sum)' will give check error results less than zero which (i) you do not want to round to zero, because it is a real error and (ii) you may mistakenly disregard as being 'only a rounding' but which could have a significant impact e.g., if total planned costs are not fully and correctly distributed across participating departments.

When rounding, always build the rounding into the check formula itself and do not round on the master data sheet (see below). This will avoid the potential situation where you have an unrounded, non-zero check result shown on a source sheet ('error') but where the overall master check nevertheless shows 'Checks OK' due to rounding there. This is confusing, can undermine confidence in the master check and you can waste time tracking down the cause.

Master check

Craig Hatmaker of Beyond Excel sums up the reason you need a master check wonderfully: 'If we have a problem anywhere, we need to know about it everywhere.'

Why? Because it would be very inefficient to regularly, manually review all the checks distributed throughout a model. A master check sheet is therefore highly recommended. Here, all check results are collected and used to calculate a master check result. The master check result is then sent to all sheets, so you can see the master check result no matter where you are in your workbook. Why? Because it would be very inefficient to have to keep going back to look at the master checks sheet and you can see immediately if a change causes an error. Then you know what (or at least where) the cause is. Also, you are less likely to forget to check when you have the immediate feedback of a master check error on the sheet you are working on.

So, how do go about implementing a master check? I am glad you asked! Let us tackle this in two steps, à la Hatmaker.

Step 1. 'Do we have a problem anywhere?'

	A	B	C	D	E	F	G	H
1	**Master Excel**							
2	Checks		20x0	20x1	20x2	20x3	20x4	20x5
3	TEUR		Actual	Plan	Plan	Plan	Plan	Plan
4	Checks not OK ③							
5								
6	**Worksheet**	**Result**						
7	Inputs		-	-	-	-	-	-
8	Value drivers		-	-	-	-	-	-
9	Fin stats	② 120	-	① (120)	120	-	-	-
10	Cockpit		-	-	-	-	-	-
11								
12	**Build-up to the master check**	**Example [Cell] Formula**						
13	1. Link to checks on source sheet	[D9] =FinStats!D8						
14	2. Calculate the result for each sheet = maximum absolute value	[B9] =MAX(MAX(C9:H9,0),-MIN(C9:H9,0))						
15	3. Calculate the master check = the max. absolute result for all sheets	[A4] =IF(MAX(MAX(B7:B10,0),-MIN(B7:B11,0))=0,"Checks OK","Checks not OK")						

To answer this question efficiently, you must first create a master check sheet, like the one above.

Layout: have a separate row for each sheet in your workbook and a separate column for each period. In accordance with best practice, these columns should be consistent across all sheets e.g., column C should always be the year 20x0.

Why is this layout recommended? If an error is detected, it is easy to identify on which sheet and in which period(s) it is i.e., where are the non-zero values? In this screenshot above: sheet Fin stats, years 20x1 and 20x2 (columns D and E).

Build-up to the master check in three steps:

1. Link to the checks on each source sheet (columns C to H) Each row represents a sheet in your workbook. I start each row with a

hyperlink to the relevant sheet. Then for each row, link to the checks on that sheet. If you have these on more than one row, simply add them up. Do not write check formulas on the master checks sheet itself: as always, formulas referring to other sheets are hard to write, review and test. Instead, put the calculations on the relevant sheets next to (or at least near) the cells being checked and simply link those check calculation(s) to the master check sheet, as you can see in the screenshot above (an example formula is shown for cell D9).

Note: Please see my video on how to create hyperlinks at *https://www.how2excel.com/en/create-hyperlinks-to-let-users-easily-jump-around-in-excel/*.

2. Calculate the result for each sheet = maximum absolute value (column B) You may be tempted to simply sum up the check results – if they are all zero, the sum is also zero, which indicates no error has been detected. However, it can be that in one period we have a -120 error and in another a +120 error, as shown in the screenshot above: two errors have been detected but the sum is zero and that approach would give you a 'Checks OK' result, which is incorrect. To avoid this risk, you should use a more complex formula, which you can see in the screenshot above. This finds the maximum, absolute error value in each row. With a -120 error in one period and +120 error in another (as in the screenshot), we get a result of 120 and a 'Checks not OK' result. Only if check values for a sheet are zero in all periods do you get a check result of zero for the sheet.

 **how2excel tip**

Use formatting to clearly highlight any non-zero values

In the above screenshot, zeros are formatted as '-' instead of '0'. This helps to emphasise any non-zero values since they are easier to spot in a block of '-'s. To do this, mark the relevant cells you wish to format, press Ctrl 1 (format cells) then proceed as explained below.

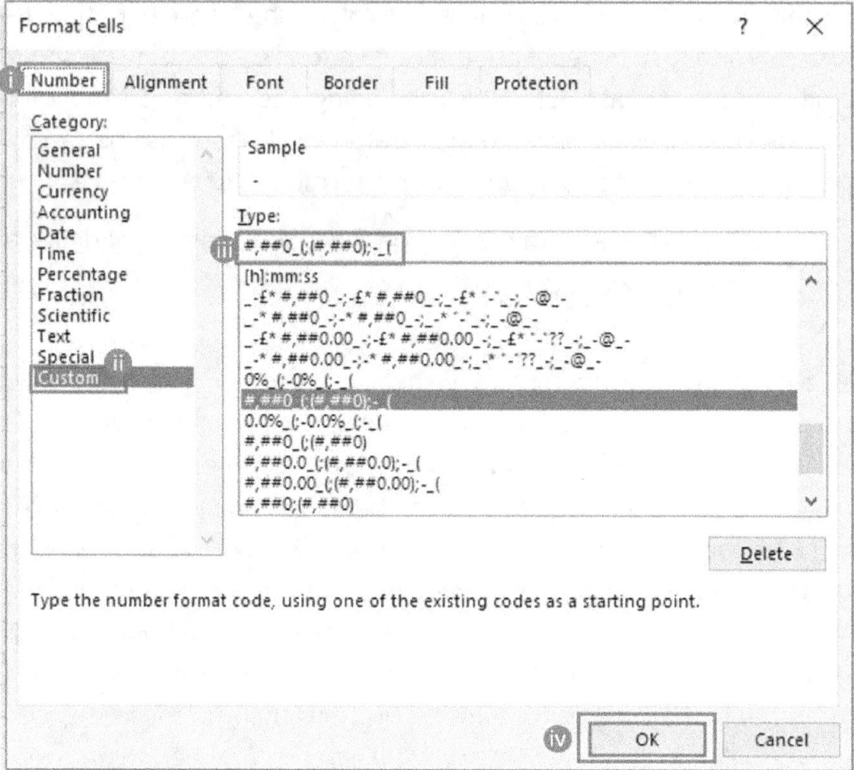

I.   Select the 'Number' tab

II.   Select 'Custom' in the list on the left

III.   In the box under 'Type' enter this (without quotes) '#,##0_(;(#,##0);-_('

This code has up to four parts, separated by semi-colons: Format for positive numbers; negative numbers; zeros; text (not defined in this example).

In the third position we see how zeros should be displayed: as a hyphen with a space afterwards (that is what the underscore character means) equal to the width of a bracket (that is the last bit of the format). This 'spacer' is used for positive numbers and zeros so that they line up with negative numbers, which are enclosed in brackets (accounting format). This makes columns of data easier to read and analyse. Which is why it is one of the four design principles: alignment. (See sub-chapter 2.3 'Rule #3 – Use a clear, clean, consistent design' for more details).

IV.   Click 'OK'

3.   Calculate the master check = the maximum absolute value for all sheets (cell A4)

The overall result of the master checks sheet should be clear and unambiguous, such as 'Checks OK' or 'Checks not OK'.

Once again, we do not sum up the sheet results (column B) but rather we find the maximum absolute value for all sheets, for the same reasons that we adopt this approach for each sheet – to avoid 'cancelling' errors not being reported as an error. If, and only if, all sheet results are zero do we report 'Checks OK'.

I use conditional formatting for this cell so that if the result is not 'Checks OK' the text is made bold and red (see sub-chapter 2.5 'Rule #5 - Write instructions of users' for more details on conditional formatting). This means a check error result should be more easily noticed.

Alternative check results

I have seen models where each individual check result is shown as either 'OK' or 'Not OK'. Since such results are text, you cannot add them up. Therefore, you must use the COUNTIF function to generate a master check result from all the individual check results, e.g., =COUNTIF(range; '<>OK'). A result of zero means there were no check results that were '<>OK', i.e., checks OK.

I prefer to calculate the difference as a number, however, because if a check fails (e.g., balance sheet does not balance) the check result doesn't just tell you there is a problem, but the value gives you valuable extra information as to the size of the error. This can help you track down and correct the cause, e.g., a check result of 120 could help remind you that a new line of data you had just inserted had a value of 120 and maybe you forgot to update a SUM formula.

Now we have our master check result, let us cover what to do with it.

Step 2. 'We need to know about it everywhere'
The master check result should be shown clearly throughout the workbook, so that a check error can be recognised immediately when it occurs, no matter which sheet you are on. Show it on the cover sheet and on all other worksheets, e.g., in cell A4, linked to cell $A$4 on the check sheet (assuming that is where your master check result is located, as in the screenshot under step 1 above). I always fix this cell reference (with dollar symbols) so it will always be correctly linked if I copy and paste it.

As on the master check sheet, I use conditional formatting for the relevant cells so that if the result is not 'Checks OK' the text is made bold and red so that a 'Checks not OK' result really jumps out at you. If you suddenly get a 'Checks not OK' result, the cause for the error should then be relatively easy to find – whatever you just changed caused the error because, before that change, the master check was OK... simple and effective!

Before closing this sub-chapter, let us briefly answer two check-related questions.

When should you add checks to your spreadsheet?
As soon as you can! I read of a large and complicated model where the balance sheet did not balance but this was not noticed until late in the model development when the checks were finally added. The developer then spent a lot of time searching for the error, was unsuccessful in finding it and finally had to rewrite a lot of the model to

get a balancing balance sheet. The moral of this story is: create your master checks sheet very early and link each check to it as you create it.

What are performance alert checks?

Up until now, I have been writing about what might be called spreadsheet integrity checks. If any of these fail (checks not OK) then you have an error which needs to be found and fixed. It is also possible to adopt similar techniques for performance alerts – these do not indicate 'formula errors' but rather 'business problems', often KPIs outside of a desired range. Typical examples here include:

- Profitability ratios including net profit ratio or return on invested capital too low

- Asset efficiency ratios such as working capital days (DSO = days sales outstanding, DIO = days inventory on-hand or DPO = days payable outstanding) are too high

- Liquidity tests such as free cash flow or cash balance below a pre-set minimum

- Debt ratios, e.g., debt service coverage or debt / (debt + equity) covenants not meeting agreed minimum or maximum values

- Project funding not completely repaid at the end of the project

See check type 5 'Values should be in expected ranges' shown above for a suggestion of how to construct such a check.

If you do not wish to do-it-yourself, Beyond Excel (BXL) offers an integrity check add-in for a small fee on eloquens, which helps you add checks to your models:

https://www.eloquens.com/tool/zQyzt7R3/finance/excel-add-ins/bxl-integrity-checks-add-in

5.2. REVIEW AND TEST YOUR SPREADSHEET

The importance of review and testing cannot be overstated. Errors are best avoided e.g., by following Golden Ground Rules, but some may still slip through the net. Review and testing gives you the chance to detect these errors so you can then find and correct them (see chapter 6 'Find and correct errors') before the model is used for its intended purpose. In practice, these activities tend to flow into each other, but we separate them into two chapters here for clarity.

A frequently asked question is: should I review and test my workbook if all checks are OK? The answer is an emphatic 'yes!' because a lack of check errors sadly does not mean the file is free of errors. So, you must review and test to detect any errors not previously detected ☺.

Review and testing can be split into the following stages:

1. Low-level

2. Medium-level

3. High-level

Each stage comprises separate review and testing activities, which are important in their own right as each has a chance to detect errors in different ways. For example, even if you notice nothing unusual in your review, there still may be errors to be found by testing, including those which only arise with alternative inputs and assumptions. Let us look at each stage in turn and find out what you need to do.

1. Low-level review and testing

When: Constantly during workbook development

Who: Workbook developer

Scope: Individual calculations, such as planned sales per period

Step 1: Review

After you first develop a calculation, you should review it. First, check the formulas that make up the calculation (which could be spread over multiple rows). Select a cell with a unique formula and review the precedents and the calculation logic (you will find details on how to do that in the next chapter 'Find and correct errors'). If you are following best practice (which of course you are, after reading this book), the precedents should be located nearby making this task a lot easier.

Step 2: Testing

Then test the results. You can change some values in the calculation to see what happens. If the calculation includes input cells, you can type in a new value for test purposes. If, however, values come from elsewhere in the model, you may find it easier to overtype such a value with a new value purely for test purposes. It is useful to test the effect of negative values, small values, large values, and also round numbers e.g., 100 or 1,000. With round numbers, it is easier to calculate or estimate the expected result in your head.

In such cases where you overtype an input or link for test purposes, you will need to revert back to the original input or formula once you have completed your testing. To reduce the risk that I forget, I mark overwritten cells in bright yellow. To reinstate an overwritten formula is easy – I just copy the formula from an adjacent cell. In order to be able to reinstate an input, I suggest you copy it to a blank cell nearby before you overwrite it. If you forgot to do that, simply undo the changes (Ctrl Z) until you get back to the original state. Alternatively, open an older, back-up copy of the workbook and copy it from there.

For more complex calculations, follow the useful mathematical concept of 'relaxation', which basically means start simple and gradually add complexity. Test a simple, basic case first, e.g., a fixed asset calculation with no planned capex. Then add one capex and review the calculation results again. Then add capex figures in multiple periods and check the results again. Then try it all again with a different estimated useful life (depreciation period in years). In this way, if you detect an error or anomaly, you can more easily identify what is causing it and can amend the calculations if necessary.

2. Medium-level review and testing

When: At significant 'milestone' points during workbook development e.g., you have just completed all sales and costs calculations and linked them into your P&L in the financial statement outputs.

Who: Workbook developer

Scope: A major workbook section, such as a complete P&L account

Step 1: Review

Once a particular workbook section is complete you should review it in its entirety. For example, you have all the P&L value driver calculations completed and linked to the P&L. You can now review the P&L in its entirety, with a focus on key numbers and trends over time.

In each case, ask yourself if the numbers make sense and are in line with both your understanding and your expectations, based upon the key inputs and assumptions. Are they steady over time, or do they show unusual or unexpected changes? If so, can you identify why? For a P&L, areas to cover in your review should include:

- **Sales:** What are the sales values and how do they develop over time?

- **Key cost positions:** Do the values appear to make sense, and how do they develop over time, both in absolute terms and in percentage of sales? Variable costs such as material and distribution costs should rise more or less in line with sales; fixed costs such as personnel and rent should rise with inflation and maybe with step ups, e.g., when you need a larger office or production site.

- **Results – Gross profit, EBITDA and net profit:** How much are you making in each period? What are the margins (percentage of sales) in each case?

how2excel tip

Create graphs with simple shortcuts

When reviewing, it can be very useful to view a row of numbers (such as sales per period) as a graph/chart to quickly identify any oddities. Simply select the cells containing the numbers you wish to review and then press F11 or Alt F1 to get an automatic graph. F11 creates this on a new worksheet, Alt F1 creates it on the same sheet. When you are finished, you can simply delete it. The graph is created with your default settings e.g., bar chart, blue. If you wish to change these defaults, then proceed as follows. Note that Excel uses the term chart instead of graph. Right-click on a chart, then click on 'Change Chart Type'. Select a chart type that you would prefer to be the default and look at the top of the 'All Charts' tab and find this chart icon, which should have a grey background. Right-click on this and click 'Set as Default Chart'.

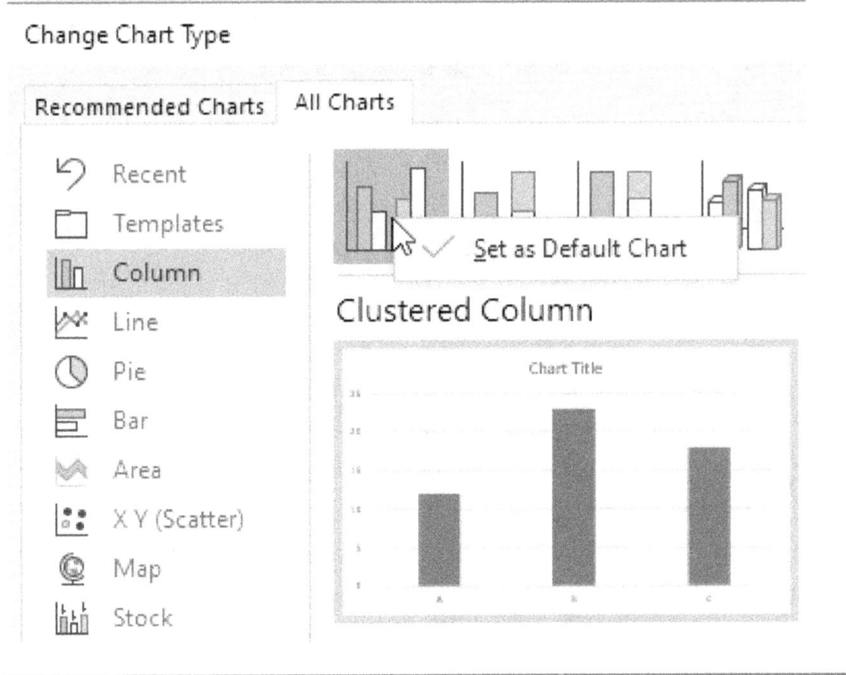

Step 2: Testing

Test odd results

For any risk areas identified (e.g., sales appear too low in later periods), trace back from the 'odd result' to the calculations and maybe back to the inputs (using the techniques that we cover in the next chapter 'Find and correct errors'). You may then need to perform low-level testing (see stage 1 above) to detect exactly where the issue is.

Perform sensitivity analysis

Try changing some key inputs or assumptions in the model and see what happens. For example, if you increase the average selling price in year 1 by (say) 10%, you should expect sales to increase 10%. If you only increased the selling price for the best-selling product that has a 20% share of sales, then you should expect only a 2% rise in total sales (10% x 20% effect). What is the effect on net operating profit? How sensitive is a particular result (say sales or profit) to a change in inputs such as price or units sold? Does a check error arise in any case where you change input data in the model? In all cases, you should clearly mark the changes you make for testing and undo these changes when you have finished, as noted previously.

 **how2excel tip**

Create a sheet back-up before major testing

If you plan to change a lot of values during your testing it can make sense to make a copy of the relevant sheet first. Select the relevant sheet tab(s), press and hold the control key and then drag the sheet tab(s) (a document symbol with a plus in it will appear) to a new location – indicated by a small black down arrow. I change the colour of the copied sheet tab to a dark pink – this is my way of marking something that should be deleted later. This copied sheet contains all

> the formulas and links of the original sheet but has no dependents so it can be safely deleted after testing… always make a back-up first though, just in case!
>
> Alternatively, you can perform such testing in a copy of the model. In both cases (copied sheet(s) or copied workbook) please remember: if you find an error, you will have to correct it in the master version, not in the copy.

3. High-level review and testing

When: Once the workbook is complete

Who: Model developer and ideally a key business user

Scope: Whole workbook with a focus on key inputs and outputs

Once the workbook is complete, you should review and test it using the techniques described above but now applied to the entire workbook with a focus on key input data, key assumptions and key outputs. A great idea here is to carry out this testing with a key business user. This has two key advantages: (i) the business user has business knowledge and can perhaps better challenge and sense-check the key assumptions and results and (ii) it starts to get them familiar with the construction and usage of the workbook – ideal for when they later start to use it on their own.

Step 1: Review

Review the workbook as a whole. What are the key results? Do these make sense, given what we know about the business or undertaking being modelled or analysed and, for plan figures, the key assumptions made. Unexpected outputs can help you identify errors – either in formulas or in assumptions – or, in some cases, give you a better understanding.

5. Detect errors

Review results of data analysis

If you are using a spreadsheet for data analysis, what are the results telling you? For example, you are analysing sales by customer this year versus last year. Are the top ten customers the same in both years? If not, who has dropped out and who are the new entrants? Does that match your knowledge and expectations? You can also use percentages, for example a Pareto distribution: what percentage of total sales do the top ten customers represent or how many customers represent 80% of sales in each year? Is there a big change year-on-year, if so why? Is there perhaps an error in the analysis?

Pivot tables are often used in data analysis work since they are very flexible and allow data to be analysed in different ways very quickly. This can help you identify insights for better business decisions. They can also help you identify errors e.g., you added new source data, but this is not reflected in the results because it is outside the data range referenced in the pivot table or possibly in SUMIF formulas.

Review financial statements

Monthly reporting packs, budgets, strategic planning models, project models and M&A models all typically contain financial statements: a P&L (at least) plus a balance sheet and cash flow statement. A review of all three components can not only help you deepen your understanding of the business or project and give you valuable insights but can also help you identify errors, either when (i) large, unexpected changes occur (e.g., why are cash flows suddenly negative?) or (ii) expected changes do not occur (e.g., when the launch of an important new product appears to have no impact on the P&L or a large capital injection appears to have no impact on the balance sheet).

Calculate and review KPIs

KPIs are great as 'sense-checkers' and can help you to identify errors – both technical (formula) errors and, for planning models, errors in planning assumptions. Develop and review KPIs as follows:

1. Decide on your KPIs, then ensure you understand them and calculate them correctly

What standard financial KPIs are useful? Typically, percentage margins are calculated for key P&L values such as gross margin, EBITDA or net profit as a percentage of sales. You can calculate such percentages for all P&L lines to give you a so-called 'common size P&L'. This enables you to compare years or divisions of different size more easily. For example, you can look at how the cost of goods sold (COGS) as a percentage of sales changes over time. If the value drops significantly, that could indicate an error unless there is a good reason e.g., the company just negotiated a new supply contract with a 5% price reduction.

Ask yourself: can I use an industry standard KPI such as revenue per available room for hotels? If so, have I understood how it is defined and have I calculated it correctly?

Are there company or group-specific KPIs I should depict? For example, one of my clients uses the term Organic Growth for the percentage change in sales revenues over the previous year and Real Internal Growth for the percentage change in sales units over the previous year. As with all KPIs, ask yourself if you have understood how it is defined and check you have calculated it correctly.

Especially if the KPI is non-standard, ask yourself: does the KPI make sense, or should I change it? For example, sales per FTE may give strange results if there are changes in non-sales departments, which do not affect sales. Perhaps it would be better to calculate sales per sales force FTE instead.

2. Perform a sense-check of the values

Do the KPI numbers appear to make sense? Can each sales force employee realistically generate (say) 500 thousand euros of sales per annum? Is this consistent with past (actual) data? If not, why not? Is the

KPI understandable or is there perhaps an unrealistic assumption, an error?

Please beware if you are using averages such as average selling price, as these can change dramatically if the sales mix changes. For example, a bakery sells filled bagels at relatively low prices to attract customers. These gained in popularity with bargain-seeking students who bought more of the low-price bagels and nothing else. Thus, total sales rose but the average selling price dropped – the sales mix had changed in favour of lower-priced bagels, which pulled down the average selling price. Such effects on averages can be particularly strong when the number of items in the group is low because relatively small changes can have large effects. There can also be a large effect if the prices vary significantly across different products, e.g., a company is selling both expensive machines and lower value machine spares. In such cases, it is probably better to analyse at a higher level such as brand, product category (here machines and spares separately) or division.

If there is a significant change in a KPI, you must ask yourself: is the change explainable or is there potentially an error?

If you are using an industry standard KPI, do the numbers make sense compared to values for competitor companies (if you can get them) or ranges of typical values stated by industry bodies or in industry reviews e.g., by one of the big four accountancy firms? Again, explainable development or potential error?

3. Review changes over time

Do the changes over time (or per country etc., dependent upon what you have calculated) appear plausible? If not, is there an explanation or is there perhaps an error?

4. Review minimum and maximum values

Are there minimum or maximum values that you expect? If so, do model values lie outside these limits in any period? If so, what inputs or assumptions do I have to change or at least challenge? For example, do I need to plan more employees (and associated costs) to support the planned levels of sales?

Review valuations

If your model includes an indicative valuation, does this appear reasonable?

If you have developed a complex model with a discounted cash flow (DCF) valuation, you can get deep in the details and may find it difficult to objectively assess this. That is why it makes sense to calculate an implied multiple e.g., EBIT multiple by dividing the DCF enterprise value by EBIT. Then you can compare this to published values for the relevant industry (e.g., in the financial press) or your own experience.

Alternatively, you can calculate one or more multiple valuations and compare the resulting values to the DCF valuation. Always ensure you are comparing enterprise values or, alternatively, equity values; do not confuse them. A peer review from an expert colleague can also be very helpful in challenging results and getting a better understanding and trust in the results or possibly identifying errors.

Review project results

Your project plan could be for a new factory, warehouse or a solar park. Do the total costs and other key results, such as time plan, make sense compared to similar projects? The Holyrood building for the Scottish Parliament was originally estimated to cost £50 million. The final cost was £414 million, and it was completed three years late. In the subsequent public inquiry, Lord Fraser commented that 'this unique one-off building could never ever have been built for £50m and I am amazed that for so long the myth has been perpetuated it could'. So, do sense-check your total costs and time plans. If your model says your project is going to be a lot cheaper and/or quicker to complete than similar projects in the past, that could be a very good sign that you should take a long, hard look at it.

5. Detect errors

Create and review graphs (called charts in Excel)

A picture paints a thousand words. That is why graphs can be so valuable in understanding and interpreting results and spotting unexpected values or changes – such tasks are often much easier with a graph than with the equivalent tables of numbers. This is true for both 'raw' numbers, like sales per year, but also for KPIs, such as sales per sales force employee or manufactured units per machine. Therefore, create graphs covering major results and KPIs. Most of these will be time-based graphs (values per year) such as:

- P&L-based: sales or profit, rental income, number of orders or customers etc.

- Balance sheet-based: development of fixed assets, working capital, debt and cash

- Cash flow: operating, investing and financing cash flows.

Graphs enable you to efficiently assess and interpret the results and possibly identify anomalies for investigation to gain a better understanding or to identify potential errors.

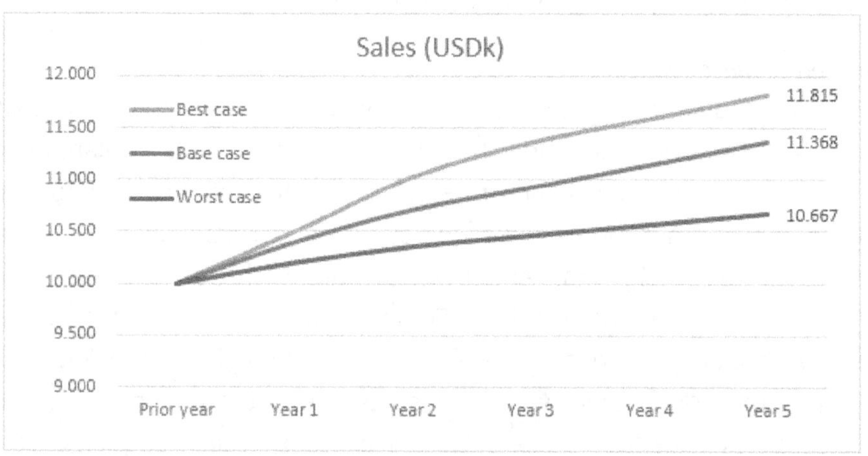

If you have various scenarios in your model, you can use a data table to generate values for each scenario and plot these on a single graph to enable comparisons (see screenshot above). Details are beyond the scope of this book, so please search online for details, if desired.

Step 2: Testing

For data analysis workbooks, use the functionality you have developed (e.g., pivot tables, result graphs, tables with filters) to analyse the data in different ways and investigate unexpected results e.g., outliers. Do they appear plausible or is there a data or formula error?

For planning models, this stage of testing is especially important to check the integrity of P&L, balance sheet, and cash flow and the interplay between them. Ask the following types of question:

- What happens if a key input or assumption is changed? For example, if sales prices are increased, do sales, profit, accounts receivable and cash balances all increase accordingly?

- If assumptions for working capital (accounts receivable, inventory and accounts payable) are changed, do relevant balance sheet positions including cash change accordingly?

- If capex is increased, does profit decrease but by a lower amount (only depreciation and tax effects) and does total cash decrease?

- Are loan drawdowns, repayments and dividend payments correctly reflected e.g., in the balance sheet (debt and equity respectively) and cash flow (financing)?

- If any results change significantly over time, are the drivers of such changes clear and reasonable?

- Do any changes result in check errors (detected via your master check), notably an unbalanced balance sheet?

Here you can once again use the very useful mathematical concept of relaxation which we already met above, and which basically means start simple and gradually add complexity. So, try testing your spreadsheet in its simplest form with base case selected, any switches turned off, no expansion capex etc. This enables you to see if the spreadsheet produces plausible results in its 'plain vanilla' version. If that seems ok, start to add in extra items and select alternative cases one at a time and test and review results after each change. I have found this approach invaluable in tracking down the cause of errors or unexpected outputs.

This type of testing may unearth not only what we may call 'technical errors' but also 'business errors' i.e., the formulas are correct, but the data and assumptions lead to undesirable results, which may require a rethink. For example, planned profit levels or cash figures are too low (or unrealistically high). Such business areas are vital to get right, especially in periods of low solvency such as trading challenges or in case of rapid expansion.

Maybe you are dealing with a new business or project. This may be expected to have losses and negative cash flows in initial periods until sales levels rise sufficiently to enable the business to cross the break-even point into profitability. But especially if the initial period of losses is long, you should look critically at the cash flow. If necessary, revise assumptions for e.g., planned capex, working capital and financing. Here it is vital to remember: changing a number in the spreadsheet does not change the real world. You must make plans to carry out the change in reality!

An existing business should be more steady-state, unless strategic changes are being planned such as the introduction of a major new product, expansion into a new geographical area or the purchase of new machinery e.g., to reduce production costs. In such cases, you need to review and test if the changes in outputs appear reasonable and reliable.

A final idea: When developing your model, it is dangerous to assume anything. But when testing your model, it can be useful to assume that your model has a material error and set yourself the goal that you will find it! Where could it be? Do any parts of your model cause you restless nights or give you a niggling doubt that they may not be 100% reliable? If so, what is the best way to test them?

5.3. GET AN INDEPENDENT REVIEW AND TEST

Finally, the complete model should ideally be reviewed and tested by another suitable person who was not involved in the model development. This person should have knowledge of and expertise in the area being analysed or modelled. Your organisation may decide that independent testing will only be carried out for more complex workbooks or if the value of the business or project being depicted is above a pre-set threshold.

Step 1: Review

Here is a list of questions an independent expert or peer can ask you to get a feel for the model:

- What is the purpose of your model? (This should be stated in brief on the cover sheet.)
- How does it fulfil this purpose?
- What are the key results and how are they (at a high-level) calculated?
- What are the main data flows in the model from inputs through to the key results?
- What input data and major assumptions did you use? For example, sales growth rates, cost inflation including pay rises and material costs, necessary capex.
- Where did these come from? (In God we trust, all others bring data!)
- Are they reliable and up-to-date?
- What checks do you have in the model and are they all 'OK'?

- Do the key results appear plausible given the key inputs and assumptions and considering all that we currently know?

- What testing have you performed on the model?

Step 2: Testing

The model developer and independent expert should perform a walkthrough of the model from inputs to results. The independent expert should then conduct their own testing as described above and using the techniques explained in chapter 5 'Find and correct errors'. They should not, however, correct any errors found but should provide details in a table or report for investigation and correction by the model developer.

Once you have (or think you may have) detected that there is an error in your spreadsheet, well done! That means you can now move on to finding and correcting it so that your model becomes more reliable. We cover this important topic in the next chapter. Before we move on, however, here is a checklist of the key points from this chapter.

5.4. BEST PRACTICE CHECKLIST

- Build in error checks throughout your model and a master check

- Review and test your content at all stages of development

- Get an independent/peer review, at least for 'high value' workbooks

6. Find and correct errors

'To rise from error to truth is rare and beautiful.'
Victor Hugo - French poet, novelist, and dramatist

I do not believe Victor Hugo ever worked on a spreadsheet, but I hope his quote will inspire you to search for and weed out any errors that may have slipped through the net of prevention.

As noted previously, I have separated 'Detect errors' (chapter 5, the previous chapter) and 'Find and correct errors' (chapter 6, this chapter) for clarity. In reality, however, there is often no clear division between the two. You may detect and find the cause of an error – such as an incorrect input – at the same time. In other cases, however, such as when the balance sheet does not balance (error detected), you will need to adopt a systematic approach to find the cause and then correct the error.

Where should you start? If you have detected a (potential) error e.g., a value that is, or appears to be, incorrect then start there. Alternatively, start with a key output that you wish to review and test. In each case, you should work back to find out how the value was calculated and what input data and assumptions were used.

A word or two on terminology: this kind of work (and it can be hard work, but it is a lot easier if best practice rules have been followed) is often referred to as a 'model audit' if applied comprehensively to a whole workbook. In addition, the actions associated with tracing calculations and data flows through a model is often also referred to as auditing and Microsoft calls its built-in Excel tools 'Formula auditing'. But the term 'auditing' can lead to misunderstandings and false expectations. If such work is performed by an independent professional organisation, you will almost certainly not get an audit certificate at the end to say, 'We have audited model XYZ.xlsx dated xx.xx.20xx and confirm that it contains no errors.' This is because there is always a risk of unidentified errors. I therefore prefer the term 'model review' but I do also use the term audit, notably when referring to the so-named Microsoft toolbar or to audit trails, a standard and useful term from the world of company accounts' auditing.

So how can you carry out a model review? Thankfully, there are a number of tools available, both standard Excel and third-party add-ins which I give a brief overview of below. Please remember, however, that

'A fool with a tool is still a fool... and a dangerous one.'

So, select relevant tools and learn to use them well.

6.1. STANDARD EXCEL

The techniques explained here will also be useful in review and testing (covered in the previous chapter 5 'Detect errors').

Review formulas in edit mode (F2)

Select a cell and press F2 to enter 'edit mode'. You can then edit or simply analyse the formula. I use this a lot which is very evident from the state of the F2 key on my keyboard! This has some useful properties for formula auditing, as follows:

	X ✓ f_x	=C2*C3/1000				
	A	B	C	D	E	F	G
1	SALES (TEUR)	Units	Year 1	Year 2	Year 3	Year 4	Year 5
2	Sales price per unit	EUR	100	104	108	112	117
3	Quantity sold	Units	10,000	10,200	10,404	10,612	10,824
4	Sales	TEUR	C2*C3/1000	1,061	1,125	1,194	1,266

Precedent cells on the same sheet are marked with coloured boxes. The colours of these boxes match the colours of the cell references in the formula bar, in the example above, blue and orange. Cell reference B2 is marked blue in the formula bar and the cell B2 has a blue box around it. You may have to scroll up or down to see the precedent cells.

If you find an error and want to correct the formula, you can amend the precedent cells or ranges by dragging and dropping the coloured boxes with the mouse. You can also change their size of ranges (e.g., in SUM formulas) using the handles (small squares) in each corner. This is one of the few cases where I find it preferable to use the mouse instead of the keyboard.

If a formula contains a function, you get useful information, as shown in the example below for MATCH.

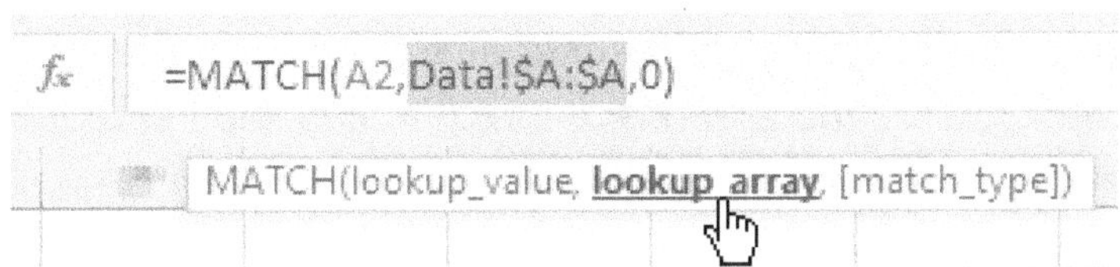

Excel shows you a so-called 'tooltip' box just below the formula bar with all the arguments listed in order. Arguments are simply the bits between the brackets – what Excel needs to know to make the function work. Any arguments shown in square brackets are optional, like [match_type] shown here. (Although optional, I strongly recommend defining this argument – usually 0 – to ensure you get a correct match.) If you want to know what option Excel uses if you do not define an optional argument, you can find out in the help files, but to avoid errors it is better to be explicit and not rely on defaults.

The tooltip appears automatically when you enter a function name and the open bracket. If a formula has already been entered, you can also get the tooltip for any function used by clicking on it in the formula bar.

If you click an argument in the tooltip and hover over it with the mouse, it is underlined and marked in bold blue, as shown in the screenshot above. If you click on this, the relevant part of the formula is selected in the formula bar. This can be very helpful in understanding and debugging a formula, especially one with nested brackets such as when you use multiple IFs. Excel allows up to 64 (nested) IF statements in a single formula but I nevertheless recommend using no more than two. If you need more, then it is often better to spread such calculations over two or more rows. This makes it easier to write and understand and so reduces the risk of error. If you need more than (say) four you can probably find a better alternative solution, possibly using INDEX or CHOOSE.

how2excel tip

Use F2 often, to review and amend formulas

When you press F2, the cursor appears as a vertical line in the formula bar at the end of the formula. You should be aware that there are two edit modes which determine what happens when you use the arrow keys on your keyboard: (i) you move the cursor around in the formula to correct or amend it by typing or (ii) if the cursor is in front of a cell reference, you can select a new (precedent) cell in the spreadsheet. You can simply toggle between the two modes by pressing F2 again. This trick also works in other cases where ranges are displayed, e.g., data validation and graph data ranges.

My opinion: This is a truly indispensable way of analysing and checking formulas. It is your friend and like all good friends, it is always there to help you. Use it often.

Background error checking

Under File, Options, Formulas you will find the error checking switch ('Enable background error checking' check box) and the error checking rules, which can be individually turned on and off using check boxes.

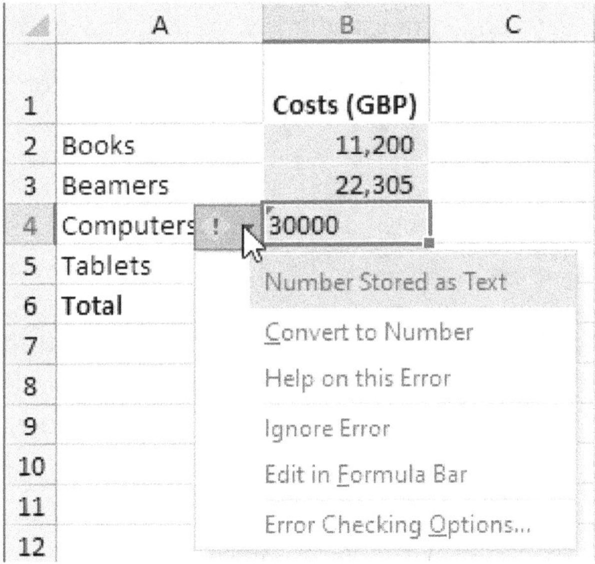

Hover with the mouse over a rule or click on the information symbol (an 'I' in a circle) for more information on it. For error checking rules that are turned on (check box is selected), Excel marks relevant 'error cells' in your spreadsheet with a small marker in the corner. By default, the marker is green. Select such a cell and you get a warning symbol and a list of options.

My opinion: These checks can be useful, but I often find there are too many 'false positives' i.e., a cell is marked as an error, but it is not, so I have turned many of them off. Please see the above screenshot to see the few options I have activated. One of these is 'Unlocked cells containing formulas'. This is useful when you protect a workbook to prevent unauthorised changes, a technique we covered in sub-chapter 2.4 'Rule #4 – Restrict access, inputs and changes'. Then Excel automatically marks any unprotected cells with a green corner. You can then turn on protection for such cells, either using Ctrl 1 (format cells), Protection tab, check the 'Locked' checkbox or (better) select a suitable cell style for the cell(s). See sub-chapter 2.3 'Rule #3 - Use a clear, clean consistent design' for more details on cell styles.

INQUIRE ADD-IN

Inquire is a standard Excel add-in but according to Microsoft it is only available in the Office Professional Plus and Microsoft 365 Apps for enterprise editions. Even if your Excel has it, it must be turned on under File, Options, Add-Ins, COM Add-Ins. According to Microsoft: 'If you don't see an entry for Inquire Add-in in the COM Add-Ins dialog box, it's because either your version of Office or Excel doesn't include it, or your organization's system administrator has made it unavailable.'

If available and turned on, Inquire offers a number of review tools.

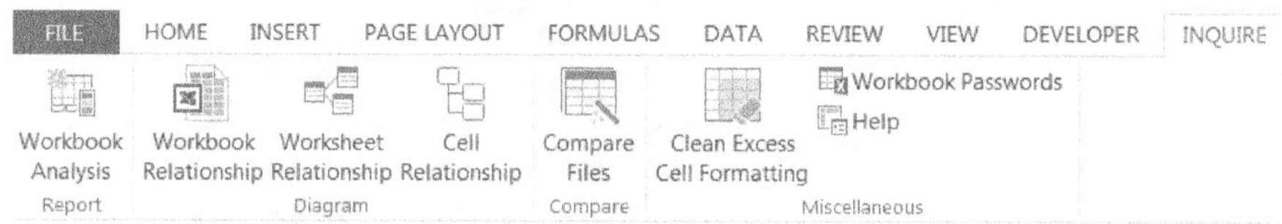

- 'Workbook Analysis' provides a long list of checks and after the name of each check, the number of such errors it has found in brackets. You can select as many as you want and export details into a separate Excel file to check in more detail. At first sight, this looks very promising, but I have found it tends to report too many false positives i.e., items which are not really errors.

- 'Workbook Relationship' shows linked external files.

- 'Worksheet Relationship' shows links between sheets within your workbook.

- 'Compare files' can be very useful if you want to compare two versions of a spreadsheet to see what has changed e.g., to identify why a particular output has changed so significantly from the prior version or to find out which data a user has changed. Both files to be compared must be open and Excel produces an interactive reporting screen split into five windows, two in the top half and three below.

In the upper two windows, you can see and navigate through the two source files. Changed cells are marked in colour to indicate the type of change: green for changed entered values (inputs), purple for changed formulas etc. In the first of the lower windows, you can select what types of changes are to be shown: inputs, formulas etc. In the next window, you see a list of the sheets and cells with changes. You can export this list to an Excel file using 'Export Results'. In the final window, you get a bar chart showing the number of changes of each type.

My opinion: As noted above, 'Workbook Analysis' has too many false positives. 'Compare Files' can be very useful if you need to perform such a check. 'Worksheet Relationship' can be useful if you have no other add-in to show you this information. Other than that, I find that third-party add-ins (see below) are often better.

Formula Auditing tools

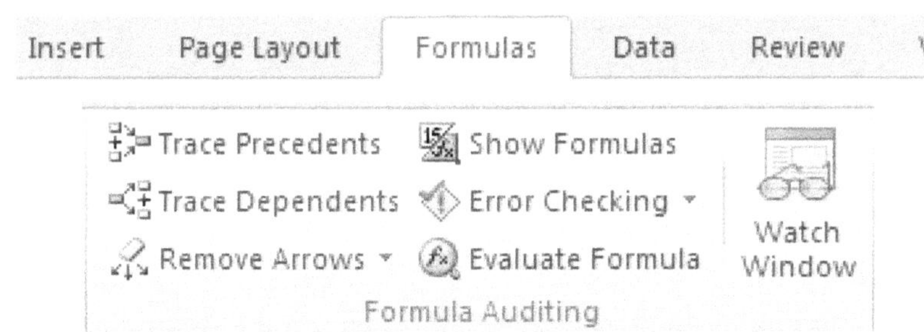

The Formula Auditing tools can be found on the formulas ribbon. There are seven tools available, some very useful, others less so.

6. Find and correct errors

Trace Precedents

Shows arrows to the cells or ranges used by the formula in the selected cell. Click 'Trace Precedents' again to identify the predecessors of the predecessors. This can be very useful. The following screenshot shows how I have done this to identify the precedents of the total sales for the year and it clearly shows that one value (Region South, Q1) is missing from the total.

	A	B	C	D	E	F
1	SALES (TEUR)	Q1	Q2	Q3	Q4	Year
2	North	194	226	175	236	831
3	South	184	186	232	171	589
4	East	130	163	104	188	585
5	West	120	198	190	207	715
6	Total	628	773	701	802	2.720

For any predecessors on the same worksheet, blue lines appear between the selected cell and precedent cell(s) and a small blue dot marks each precedent cell, as can be seen in the screenshot above. It can be tricky to see these small blue dots when two or more precedents lie in exactly the same direction, e.g., in the same column as the selected cell, so take care.

how2excel tip

Use 'Trace Precedents' in combination with F2

In such cases, press F2 to enter edit mode. The predecessor cells then have a blue dot AND a coloured box (while you remain in edit mode), so are much easier to find. You can double-click on a blue line to jump between the analysed cell and a predecessor cell.

Predecessors on other sheets are indicated by a black, dashed line with an arrowhead. Double-click on the dashed line to open a list of precedent cells, then double-click on a selected

> precedent to jump to it. To return to the original cell, press F5 (opens the Go To – Window and has the last modified cell preselected) then Enter (this is such a super tip, I cover it again in more detail below). You can then go through the process again to examine another precedent.

This functionality is very useful but also frustrating for off-sheet precedents, for three main reasons:

1. Each off-sheet precedent is listed with the full file name, then sheet name and finally cell range. You cannot expand the dialog box. So, unless you have a very short file name then you usually cannot see the precedent descriptions in full, which makes it hard to use e.g., to identify all sheets on which a cell is referenced. If you follow best practice, then your formulas are short and have limited off-sheet links, but tracing precedents in this way can nevertheless be a pain. I can, however, offer two tips here.

 **how2excel tips**

Understand the order of precedents shown

- The order of the precedents in the list is exactly the same order as they appear in the formula. If you only have, say, five off-sheet precedents, you can relatively easily tell which is which.

- You can rename your file before reviewing to a very short name such as 'Plan'. This makes it much easier to see more of the precedents and dependents listed in the relevant dialog box.

2. You have to double-click the dashed arrow to open the list each time and then double-click on the (next) precedent.

3. If the precedent happens to be in a row or column which is either hidden (not best practice but it happens) or simply in a closed row or column grouping, then you can't see what it is without unhiding or ungrouping each time.

For these reasons, I recommend that you use an add-in, such as MacAbacus Lite (see below). You can also use my how2excel tips for precedents, see below.

Trace Dependents

Similar to trace precedents above, but traces links in the other direction to answer the question: where is the data going? If a cell has no dependents but is also not an output then this suggests there could be a linking error. Find the cell which you think it should be linked to (e.g., an output sheet) then check the formula there.

Here the disadvantage of the small, non-expanding dialog with the list of dependents is often much worse than for precedents, since data used in SUMIFS, INDEX, MATCH or VLOOKUP will often have many dependents. The list of dependents is unclear because you cannot see the full 'name' of the dependents including cell reference (see the screenshot in the tip below).

 **how2excel tip**

Use the mouse to read the complete precedent

Select one precedent from the list, so it appears in the 'Reference' field below and then use the mouse to select the text shown to the very end so you can see the dependent sheet name and cell reference.

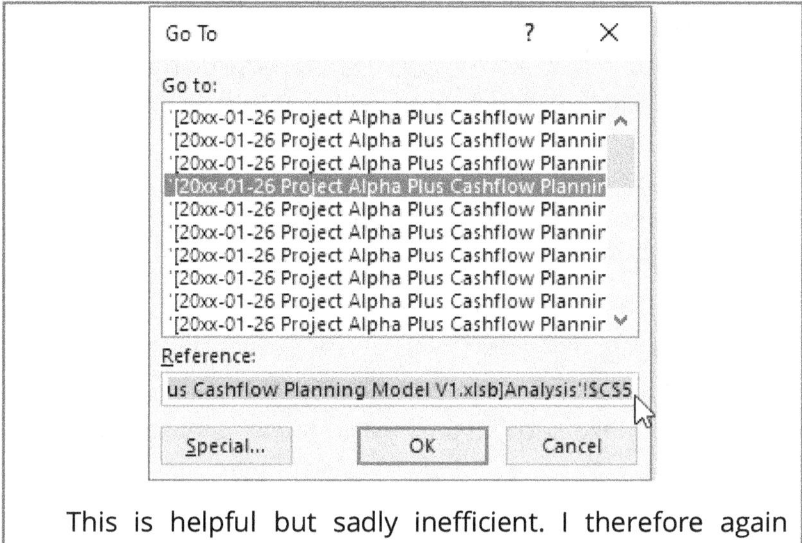

This is helpful but sadly inefficient. I therefore again recommend that you use an add-in (see below). You can also use my how2excel tip for dependents, see below.

Remove Arrows

All drawn arrows will be removed. Alternatively, simply save the model. You should probably do this before starting each new data flow analysis to avoid getting confused between different data flows.

Show Formulas

Shows the formulas for all cells instead of the calculated values. This can be very helpful to see if someone overtyped a formula with a value. When in this mode, all precedent cells on the same sheet are marked with coloured boxes, the same as when you press F2 in 'normal view', which can be useful.

To enter 'show formulas mode', you can instead use the keyboard shortcut Ctrl Shift ` (three keys all at the same time). Press the combination again to return to 'normal' mode.

Error Checking

Only works for technical errors such as #DIV/0. Describes the type of error in the current cell, gives details about it, and allows you to find the predecessors. Trace to error attempts to determine the error-causing cells but is not always successful, particularly if the cause is complex.

Evaluate Formula

A great function! The formula in the cell is evaluated step-by-step. This can help you better understand the calculation logic and identify possible errors, for example a misplaced or missing bracket. Works best if the formula is relatively short, which is best practice. This tool may give you the final nudge you need to break down a complex formula over several rows to make each step easier to follow and reduce the risk of error.

With nested functions, 'drill-down' is possible so you can see how a referenced cell in your formula is calculated without having to go to that cell and run the tool again.

Watch Window

Allows you to track values in defined cells to determine the impact of changes (e.g., input or assumptions). I find this useful in valuation models, where I can 'watch' the main valuation result cell and see how it changes when I change inputs or assumptions.

My opinion: Formula Auditing Tools include some of the best built-in tools; I use it a lot especially Trace Precedents and Evaluate Formulas.

 **how2excel tips**

1. Jump to first precedent simply by double-clicking

You do not necessarily need to use the 'Trace Precedents' button; you can instead use one of my all-time favourite Excel tips! You can jump to the (first) precedent cell by double-clicking on the cell. To get back again, press F5 (Go To, the cell address of the original cell appears by default) and then press enter or click OK. This only works for the first precedent of a formula, but it is nevertheless a super tip. For this tip to work, you must have the 'edit directly in cell' option turned off, as shown below. You can get to this dialog under File, Options.

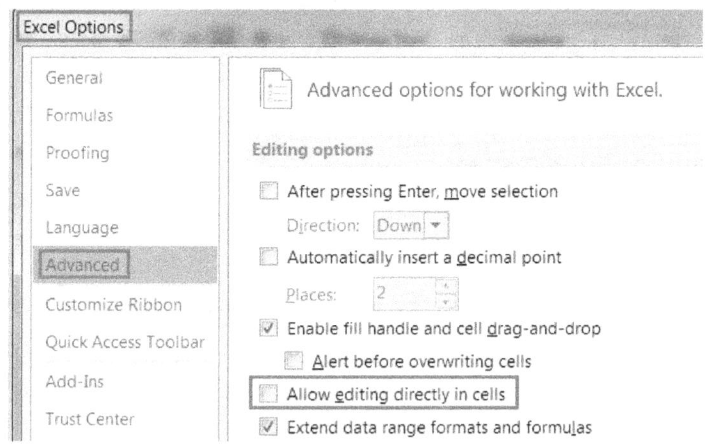

Note: For a helpful video explaining this tip, please visit *https://www.how2excel.com/en/simply-double-click-to-jump-to-cell-formula-precedent/*

2. Trace dependents using large value inputs

If you want to trace the impact of an input cell quickly and easily (e.g., to check where it flows to in the P&L and maybe to test for double counting or incorrect period linking) there is a simple trick that does not need the 'Trace Dependents' button. First, copy the correct value in the input cell to a nearby unused cell so you can change it back afterwards (or else you must rely on Ctrl Z to undo the change). Change the input to a large number such as 999999999999. This is too long for Excel to show in the cell and so you see a row of hash symbols '########' instead. All the dependents of this cell will also be shown as a row of hash symbols. Thus, you can quickly see which values are affected. Simple and effective! Remember to change the amended cell back to its original value or formula when you are finished.

6.2. THIRD-PARTY TOOLS

There are plenty of third-party tools available to help you review spreadsheets. They are generally add-ins: once installed you get an extra tab on your Excel ribbon with extra tools. Let us have a quick look at a few of these add-ins, with a focus on the features that I find particularly useful for spreadsheet reviewing.

First and foremost I am interested in a more efficient way of understanding formulas and tracing precedents. As noted above, the standard Excel Auditing toolbar has the very useful trace precedents but this is cumbersome to use. I therefore prefer to use one of the various add-ins such as MART, Arixcel or MacAbacus. Let us look briefly at MacAbacus.

Macabacus add-in

https://www.macabacus.com/features

There used to be a free version ('Lite'), but this no longer appears to be available. There is also a full version with more features. Here I look at the Lite version, which I already had.

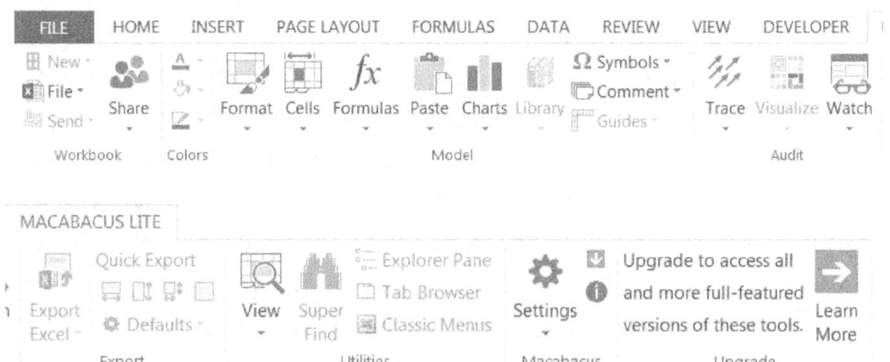

The add-in comprises a large toolbar (split in two in the above screenshots) with lots of tools, a few of which appear to be simply links to standard Excel functions gathered together in one place. The feature I use most is Trace –> Precedents Lite.

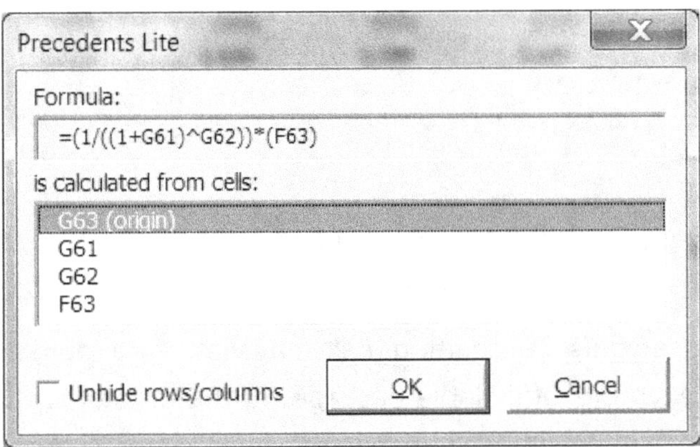

This shows you the cell formula at the top and all precedents are listed line-by-line below. You just have to click on one to jump to it – fantastic! You can select the option 'Unhide rows/columns' if one or more precedents are grouped or hidden (rememeber: it is not best practice to hide rows or columns, use groupings where necessary).

My opinion: The precedents tool is great for model reviewing and there are plenty of additional tools including non-standard graphs which may also prove useful. The pro version of Macabacus offers better functionality and ease of use. Alternative tools such as MART or Arixcel also offer precedent tracers.

The second type of review assistance on offer by third-party tools is reports. Perhaps the most well-known of these is OAK which you have to buy. You can, however, try before you buy, to see if you like it first. Alternatively, there is the free add-in from Numeritas called nXt. These differ in functionality, but both offer summaries and maps, essential reports for Excel reviewing, which I therefore explain later. So, what can these two add-ins do? Let us take a look...

OAK (Operis Analysis Kit) add-in

https://www.operisanalysiskit.com/

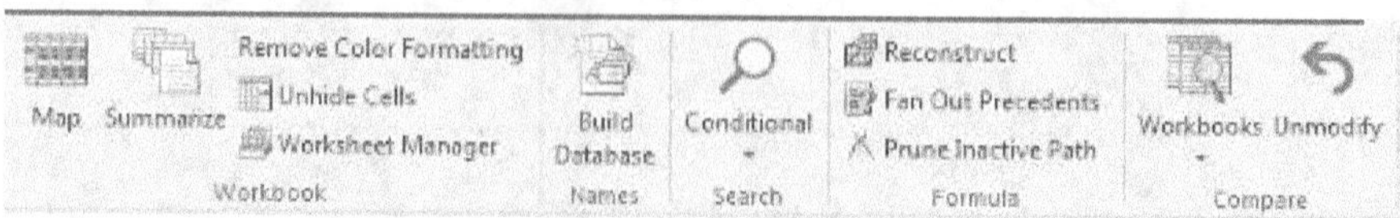

Because this add-in is so well-known, it sets the standard for competitor products. It costs money and is available in two versions:

OAK Essentials: This edition makes available the four key functions of OAK in a simple, affordable package. At the time of writing, it costs £95.

- Map: Provides a visual representation of the model's formula consistency. You can thus easily identify inconsistent formulas, which can often represent errors (see below for more details).

- Summarise: Generates reports on a model's complexity as well as modelling risk factors.

- Search: Locates cells with specific attributes.

- Compare: Indicates what has changed between versions of a workbook/worksheet/range. Equivalent functionality is available in the standard Excel add-in Inquire (see above) if this is available in your version of Excel.

OAK Professional: In addition to the four Essentials tools, the full edition of OAK provides another 28 advanced functions. At the time of writing, it costs £395, or less if you buy three or more licences.

You can install the tool for a free 30-day trial.

My opinion: OAK is a professional tool, and the reports are generally very good.

Numeritas nXt add-in

http://www.numeritas.co.uk/free-software

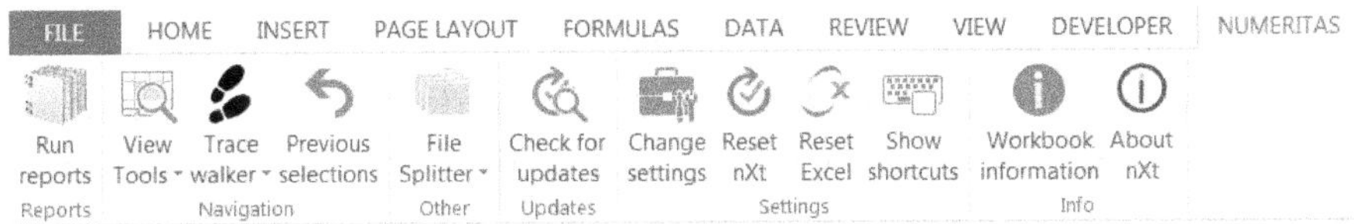

This is a free add-in from Numeritas which offers a number of reports:

- Workbook summary: Gives you information about each sheet in your workbook including the number of unique formulas etc.

- Unique formula listing: This lists every single unique formula in your workbook and provides additional information about each one.

- Workbook map: This is a visual representation of unique and consistent formulas, similar to maps in OAK (again, see below for more details).

- External links in formulas: This will list all external links found in formulas.

- External links in other items: This will check for external links in named ranges etc.

It can also run a number of checks each time you open a workbook such as whether iterations are turned on, which can be useful. It also offers keyboard shortcuts and other potentially useful tools. If you click on 'Show shortcuts' you get a new workbook with two worksheets. The second of these lists known limitations of the tool, which you should review.

My opinion: Great value for free! Worksheet maps are fundamental to model reviewing and some of the other functionality, notably the checks on opening a file, is also useful.

Key review reports

As noted above, both OAK and nXt offer a summary report and maps. A list of unique formulas can also be useful. While not wishing to write a user manual for the add-ins (that is the job of the respective developers), it is useful to briefly look at some of the key types of report so that you can better assess how useful these are, and to guide you when selecting the add-in(s) you wish to use.

Summary

Lists all worksheets in the file with statistics which can typically include:

- Total number of cells used.

- Number of formulas.

- Number of unique formulas: In well-designed worksheets this number should be no more than 20% of all formulas. If any sheets have a higher percentage, it may be worth focussing on those in your review as this can indicate a higher risk of errors (cover sheets or other sheets with little content such as separator sheets are exceptions to this rule).

- Number of inputs: If you have any inputs on output sheets, these may represent errors. In any case, consider moving them to an input sheet to comply with best practice: keep inputs, calculations and outputs separate.

- Number of cells with text.

- Number of blank cells: You may be surprised to see that over a third of cells are generally blank. If this is not the case, you may be able to improve the readability and hence user-friendliness of such sheets by adding blank rows to create what designers call white space.

List of unique formulas

Lists all unique formulas in the workbook by worksheet, stating the cell reference where each one first appears. As a general rule, longer, more complicated formulas have a higher risk of error. You can therefore use this report to focus your review on such formulas with a view to (i) simplifying where possible e.g., by spreading calculations over multiple rows and (ii) checking that such formulas are correct.

Please bear in mind, however, that while a unique formula may give a correct result in one cell, it may not do so for all other cells containing the same formula e.g., if a lookup formula has been accidentally copied into the final row in a block of calculation cells that should simply contain a total (SUM).

Maps

I find these reports are the most useful. Map reports create a new workbook with a 'map worksheet' for every worksheet in your workbook which enables you to find inconsistencies, especially in formulas. Such cells have a higher risk of error. Let us look at a small example using an nXt map.

	A	B	C	D	E	F
1	SALES SENSITIVITY					
2						
3		Sales (EUR) per m² p.a.				
4	Store size (m²)	1,000	2,000	3,000	4,000	5,000
5	100	100,000	200,000	300,000	400,000	500,000
6	200	200,000	400,000	600,000	800,000	1,000,000
7	300	300,000	500,000	900,000	1,200,000	1,500,000
8	400	400,000	800,000	1,200,000	1,600,000	2,000,000
9	500	500,000	1,000,000	1,500,000	2,000,000	2,500,000
10	600	600,000	1,200,000	1,800,000	2,400,000	3,000,000
11	700	700,000	1,400,000	2,100,000	2,800,000	3,500,000
12	800	800,000	1,600,000	2,400,000	3,200,000	4,000,000
13	900	900,000	1,800,000	2,700,000	3,600,000	4,500,000
14	1,000	1,000,000	2,000,000	3,000,000	4,000,000	5,000,000

6. Find and correct errors

In the screenshot above you can see the original worksheet which calculates **sales sensitivity**. Down column A we have various store sizes in square metres and across the columns we have potential sales in euros per square metre of store size. The table then calculates what are the expected sales in each case equal to sales per square metre times store size. At first glance the table looks OK.

Below you see the nXt map of the same worksheet plus the colour key. The colours are garish but do not affect the report content.

Map key © Numeritas

Cell A1 in the map represents cell A1 in the worksheet, cell A2 in the map represents cell A2 in the worksheet and so on. In nXt the colours used are: grey for text, yellow for values (inputs), purple for unique formulas and various shades of green for copied formulas (same as the formula to the left and/or above). Ideally, we want to see one unique formula in the top left cell of a calculation block (purple) followed by a sea of green to the right and below meaning the formula is the same in all cells. The above map looks mostly OK except for cell C7, which is yellow, indicating that it contains a value (an input). When we check the spreadsheet, we find that someone overtyped the formula with a hard-coded value of 500,000, which is both incorrect and not best practice. You can then correct this by copying the formula from the cell above. I think you will agree that this kind of report is very useful for finding errors as it dramatically speeds up the review for inconsistencies, which can often indicate errors.

You can also find this kind of error using standard Excel, but it is harder work. You can use the formula view (explained above under the Excel Auditing toolbar). Alternatively, you can select the block of cells, press F5 (Go To), special, constants, OK. Excel then marks the cells which are not formulas, in this case just the cell C7. These approaches may be OK for small worksheets but are not efficient for larger workbooks. Therefore, map reports win hands down for efficiency.

6.3. CONCLUSIONS

To sum up, you should get to know the standard Excel tools and also install and use one or more third-party add-ins to help you review your own models or those of your colleagues.

If you find errors in your own spreadsheet, you should obviously correct them. It is a different case when you find errors in someone else's spreadsheet. Here I suggest you do not correct the errors yourself. For one thing, you would probably not want someone else to amend your spreadsheet, at least not without your permission. Secondly, you may not have a full understanding of the model (maybe it is not an error after all, you just did not understand something fully) or you may not be aware of other areas of the spreadsheet that may also need changing as a result. And lastly, you may no longer have the latest version of the file. Therefore, I suggest that you create a list of your findings (in Excel, of course) for your colleague to go through and correct, as necessary.

Such a list should include the following columns:

- **Number** (optional): A sequential number to facilitate discussion or comments e.g., in e-mails.

- **Worksheet**: The worksheet where you found the potential error.

- **Cells**: The relevant cell, column, row or range.

- **Finding**: Details of the potential error or finding which you identified.

- **Suggestion:** What should be done to rectify the finding (optional).

- **Priority:** high, medium, or low (alternatively 1 to 3, but then be very sure to make it clear whether 1 is high or low!) High priority findings have (or could have) a high impact, medium findings a medium impact and low findings a low or no impact. Here we are generally talking about the actual or potential impact on key results (i.e., spreadsheet reliability) but you could also record findings if you identify improvements for model understanding or ease or use. If time or budget is limited, you may choose to ignore low priority findings and not record them.

- **Status:** open, corrected, rejected – this allows tracking of progress and also filtering when the spreadsheet developer reviews the findings to update the spreadsheet. They can filter the list to show only high priority, open findings and deal with those first.

- **Comments**: A column for the developer to record why a finding does not represent an error (optional).

For ease of review by the spreadsheet developer, I always sort my findings by worksheet (starting with findings for the left-most sheets in the file and moving on to other sheets to the right) and then by row and/or column.

6.4. BEST PRACTICE CHECKLIST

- Learn to use both the standard (built-in) tools and third-party tools to help you review and test your workbooks and also to find errors in them.

- Try out various third-party tools to find ones which you find effective; as a minimum, these should offer better precedent tracing and maps.

7. How to excel

'Use it or lose it'
Time-tested idiom, which I use at the end
of all my training courses

So, now you have learnt how to excel at creating reliable, flexible and user-friendly spreadsheets. The Golden Ground Rules give you the fundamental basis to succeed. You can help avoid horror stories, and errors in general, by being aware of potential issues and following the advice given. Combine all this with built-in checks and plenty of reviews and testing to detect and then correct any errors that may slip through. These are all learnable processes and skills. Implement them in your daily spreadsheet work and make them a habit. And please also remember to use the valuable how2excel tips. They can be fun and should make your Excel life easier according to the motto: work smarter not harder!

To help you on your way, you will find below a complete checklist of all the main tips from the book organised by book chapter. You can also download this checklist as a convenient PDF available at https://www.knott-consulting.com/en/book/ which you can print out for reference and add notes to if you wish. If you need to refresh your memory on any point, then please refer to the relevant chapter in the book.

I wish you success with your spreadsheets. If you found the advice in this book useful, please pass it on to other spreadsheet developers and users, so we can improve the quality of all spreadsheets, for better decision making everywhere!

Chapter 1: Be prepared

- Decide if a spreadsheet is the best solution

- Get trained

- Plan your spreadsheet and consider:

  - Purpose and scope

  - Users

  - Language

  - Reporting currency and units

  - Time, budget and data available

  - Content and functionality

  - Period structure

- Document your design

Chapter 2: Follow Gary's Golden Ground Rules

Rule #1 – Use a clear, logical workbook structure

Decide what worksheets you need, give them clear names and get them in order.

- Spread content logically over clearly named worksheets

- Separate inputs, calculations and outputs

- Organise worksheets into sections to reflect data flow from inputs to outputs

- Include a cover sheet, ideally with hypertext links to facilitate navigation

Rule #2 – Keep your worksheets as clear and simple as possible

Ensure each worksheet is clearly laid out and easy to use.

- Use a logical structure within each worksheet

- Use consistent columns, row, formulas and whole sheets

- Formulas

    - Ensure calculations flow from left to right and from top to bottom

    - Use the KISS principle: keep it short and simple

    - Follow formula priorities: (i) correct, (ii) understandable and (iii) short

    - Follow the COUNT principle: Calculate Once, Use Numerous Times

Rule #3 – Use a clear, clean, consistent design

Ensure the whole workbook has a clear, professional look and feel.

- Use consistent (company-defined) fonts, colours and styles

- Use the four key design principles: contrast, repetition, alignment and proximity

- Clearly mark all inputs, for example as grey cells

- Minimise non-data ink e.g., borders

Rule #4 – Restrict access, inputs and changes

Ensure that only authorised users can access and change your spreadsheet and that inputs are valid.

- Restrict access to the spreadsheet using folders with restricted access and passwords

- Use data validation where relevant to help ensure inputs are valid

- Consider protecting workbooks so that changes can only be made in input cells

Rule #5 – Write instructions for users

Ensure that users know what to do and in what order e.g., how to update the model with new data.

- Create a worksheet with an action list for users to follow

- Add a status column to ensure progress is clear

Chapter 3: Learn from horror stories

Get the basics right

- Decide if a spreadsheet is the right tool for the job

- Do not be complacent and think 'it will never happen to me'

- Get trained or use suitably trained staff

- Follow the Golden Ground Rules

- Always review and test your spreadsheets and ideally have someone else do that as well (so-called 'four eyes principle')

Mistakes in usage

- Organise your data well

  - Do not use hidden rows or hidden columns or otherwise hide data; use row/column groupings

  - If appropriate, group data into separate blocks

  - Consider extra column(s) for filtering

- Special tips for sensitive/confidential data

- Be aware of the risks

- Separate such data from the rest; if appropriate, store such data in a separate file with restricted access

- Never send or publish Excel files with pivot tables based on sensitive/personal data; do not rely on pivot table options to protect this data

- If you want to send or publish aggregated results (only), use PDFs or create a 'sent version' with only outputs and no data details; break all links to source files

- Use clear version control to ensure only the latest version of a spreadsheet file is used

  - Store spreadsheets on the server or in the cloud (OneDrive) and do not send via e-mail if you can avoid it

  - Use an agreed folder structure and an agreed model naming convention

  - If files are sent back and forth, be clear who has the 'master version'

Incorrect inputs

- Get the basics right

  - Know your business and train your users

  - Implement checks early in your spreadsheet development

  - Implement controls also in the surrounding processes e.g., expert review

- Organise your inputs and source documents

  - Obtain and store source documents

  - Clearly mark input data and quote your sources

- Avoid input errors

- Follow the Golden Ground Rules, notably #4

- Choose a suitable standard currency and unit for monetary values in your workbook and use it consistently throughout e.g., thousands of US dollars

- Only vary from the standard unit for good reason, and in such cases (i) clearly state the units used and (ii) always use the standard unit for results

- Use clear labelling including units

- Define and use a sign convention, e.g., income and cash inflows positive, costs and cash outflows negative, all balance sheet values generally positive

- Construct your spreadsheet to reduce the risk of sign errors, e.g., inputs generally positive or use separate rows for positive and negative number inputs

- Clearly mark any missing, uncertain or unknown inputs, for example, you can make the text red or the background yellow; review and update these before spreadsheet completion

- Use data validation

- Do not 'right align' cells with numbers or dates because this hide text numbers that you want to identify and correct

- Convert any numeric data stored as text to numbers: either multiply by one or use 'convert text to columns'

- Check for errors

  - Increase the visibility of significant inputs by showing them on the dashboard or cockpit

  - Use Excel background checks ('green corners')

  - Add checks on your totals

- Check, validate and sense-check your inputs: ideally, get someone else to check them too

- Review your results and if possible, compare to prior data: large, odd results or variances could indicate incorrect inputs

Hard-coded values

- Do not hard-code

- Always show data, assumptions, adjustments and factors clearly as inputs

- Clearly mark any temporary hard-coding used for test purposes and remove after testing

SUM and other calculation errors

- Use AutoSum, AutoAverage etc. to help you select the correct range but always check the range selected by Excel; in particular, watch out if you have gaps in your data

- For added rows (or columns) of data:

  - Avoid adding new data above the first data row or below the last data row as these may well be excluded from the SUM

  - Use automatic range extension (Excel 2013 onwards) for rows added at the end

  - Alternatively, insert a blank line before the total and include this in the range for SUM, AVERAGE etc. so that row insertions at the end of the data are always included in the selected range

- Use an Excel table: new entries are automatically included in SUMs etc. and formulas are automatically copied to new rows

- Keep data and calculations together for clarity

  - Keep formulas next to the data used

- Avoid cross-sheet calculations - use simple links only

- Avoid mathematical errors

    - Establish and use a sign convention consistently (already recommended)

    - Understand mathematical operator precedence: BODMAS = brackets, order (power of), division/multiplication, addition/subtraction

- Use the Warren Buffet rule of modelling: only model what you understand; if necessary, ask a subject-matter expert to assist you

- As always, test your model and review your results

- Interpretation: Even if your ranges and formulas are correct, always remember that correlation does not prove causality

Copy & paste and cut & paste errors

- General tips

    - Reduce the need for copy and paste actions e.g., by keeping everything you need in one file

    - Reduce the need for cut and paste actions by using alternative functionality such as sorting, filtering and ranks or dynamic arrays, if available

    - Do not use hidden rows or columns: these can be easily overlooked when copy & pasting, cut & pasting and analysing

- Copying data

    - Paste as values, not formulas

    - Ensure source and destination areas have the same structure and consider protecting sheets to prevent structural changes

    - Copy and paste the correct rows and columns: This is best achieved using range names

- Copying formulas

    - Test your calculations, especially if a section is to be copied; test it thoroughly to be as sure as you can that it is free of material error

    - Learn and correctly use $ cell-fixing (anchoring): as a general rule, fix as much as necessary but as little as possible

    - Check your data in sections copy-pasted from somewhere else: are inputs and assumptions valid for the new area?

Incorrect links

- Follow Golden Ground Rules #2 and #3 to ensure simplicity and consistency and so reduce the risk of in-sheet and cross-sheet link errors

- Add checks e.g., to test if totals on input and calculation sheets agree in actual periods, where there should be no difference

- Avoid or minimise links to external files

Circular errors and mistakes in logic

- General tips

    - Build in error checks where possible

    - Never do calculations in output sheets other than plus/minus, SUM and possibly simple KPIs

    - Calculate KPIs to act as sense-checkers

- Circular references

    - Design calculation logic in order to avoid circular references

    - Be aware of potential issues caused by using the iterations option or copy-paste macros

- Mixing up real and nominal figures or different currencies

- Understand the terms real and nominal

- As a general rule, always calculate and use nominal numbers (i.e., including inflation effects)

- Agree on and clearly state the currency and units in use

- Double counting

  - Understand how double counting can occur

  - Calculate figures for the outputs in the same order as the outputs; if you break this rule, only do so for a valid reason and make it clear

Chapter 4: Avoid common function errors

- VLOOKUP and HLOOKUP: Avoid these functions and use XLOOKUP, INDEX and MATCH, or SUMIFS instead

- INDEX and MATCH: Ensure INDEX and MATCH ranges use the same rows (or columns)

- SUMIF/SUMIFS:

  - As a rule, use SUMIFS in preference to SUMIF, to avoid a change in the order of arguments if you add more criteria

  - Ensure sum range and criteria range use the same rows (or columns)

- NPV: Ensure there are no gaps in your cash flows; do not discount cash flows at time zero

- IRR: Be aware of the limitations of IRR, most notably that it takes no account of size; use modified versions XIRR and MIRR if appropriate and do not use IRR on its own, only in addition to other results, typically NPV

- IFERROR: Avoid using IFERROR if you can, use with caution if you can't, as it can hide errors that you should know about and correct; instead, test for the potential error e.g., the divisor is zero

Chapter 5: Detect errors

- Build in error checks throughout your model and a master check

- Review and test your content at all stages of development

- Get an independent/peer review, at least for 'high value' workbooks

Chapter 6: Find and correct errors

- Learn to use both the standard (built-in) tools and third-party tools to help you review and test your workbooks and also to find errors in them.

- Try out various third-party tools to find ones which you find effective; as a minimum, these should offer better precedent tracing and maps.

Finally, please use the how2excel tips scattered throughout the book or on https://www.how2excel.com I wish you success on your journey:

How to excel at creating reliable, user-friendly spreadsheets.

References

Beales, R. (2014). Excel in the 21st century. *Breaking views,* https://www.ft.com/content/e1f343ca-e281-11e3-89fd-00144feabdc0.

Dobelli, R. (2013). *The art of thinking clearly, chapter 15.* Harper non-fiction.

F1F9 CDS. (n.d.). *Capitalism's Dirty Secret.*

F1F9 DD. (n.d.). *Dirty Dozen - 12 Modelling Horror Stories and Spreadsheet Disasters.*

Giles, C. (2014). Piketty findings undercut by errors. *Financial Times,* https://www.ft.com/content/e1f343ca-e281-11e3-89fd-00144feabdc0.

Hermans, F. (2015). *Enron's Spreadsheets and Related Emails: A Dataset and Analysis.*

IBM. (2020). *Cost of a Data Breach Report.* https://www.ibm.com/security/data-breach.

Laidlaw, S. (2012). *Report of the Laidlaw Inquiry.* London: Controller of Her Majesty's Stationery Office.

Panko, R. (2008). *Spreadsheet Errors: What We Know. What We Think We Can Do.*

Panko, R. (2014). *Human Error in Simple but Nontrivial Cognitive Actions.* http://www.panko.com/HumanErr/SimpleNontrivial.html.

Panko, R. (2015). *What we don't know about spreadsheet errors today.* http://www.panko.com/.

Shueh, J. (2014, March 3). Retrieved from Government Technology: https://www.govtech.com/data/Why-Spreadsheets-Stink-4-Ways-to-Improve-Them.html

Tracy, B. (2014). *Time Management.*

Tufte, E. R. (2007). *The visual display of quantitative information.* Graphics Press LLC.

Index